The **Journeyman**
Larry Rinker

To Jim,

Keep Swingin!

Larry Rinker

TESTIMONIALS

"Larry Rinker will rock your world as his story of perseverance in life and his rise to the highest level of golf instruction is a true inspiration. Well done, my friend."

~ *Gary McCord, PGA Tour Veteran Member, CBS Announcer*

"This is such a killer book! Professional golf is a battle, but I never knew what was going on inside a competitor's head. All these years later, this book gives me that insight. Throughout his playing career, which overlapped with mine and allowed me to get to know him well, Larry was a student of the game. He's seen the best and played with the best, and used those experiences to become a fantastic instructor. This is a must read for anyone interested in what it takes to succeed in the cutthroat world of professional sports. I couldn't put it down."

~ *Paul Azinger, former PGA Champion and NBC Golf Analyst*

"Larry Rinker comes from perhaps the most successful golfing family in history. His passion for golf and music has helped him to understand effortless power and flow. Enjoy the read."

~ *Dr. Bob Rotella, Sports Psychologist*

"I've known Larry for over 30 years and I've always admired his ability to connect with people. It served him well as a Tour player – and it hits home again as a rising star in the teaching ranks. He may have called himself "The Journeyman" – but as anyone will tell you, the joy in life is in the journey, and no one tapped into that joy more than Larry."

~ *Jim Nantz, CBS Sports*

"Larry and I share a common bond: He happens to love music as passionately as I do the game of golf, so we were destined to be friends. For over 30 years we have been just that. I have always enjoyed Larry's company and admired his talents both on the golf course and on the bandstand. "The Journeyman" is a great perspective on the life of a Tour player. Love ya Rink."

~ *Vince Gill, 21 Grammy Awards, Country Music Hall of Fame*

TESTIMONIALS

"I've known Larry Rinker for probably 40 years. In addition to our PGA Tour connection, many of my five kids are similar in age to Larry and his siblings, and they played a lot of junior golf together in South Florida. Larry has always been a good player, but more important, Larry was able to take what he learned playing the game and competing at the highest level, and use it to teach other people and make them better golfers. Larry is a good man and a fun guy to be around. His easy-going personality allows him to connect with people and serves him well when working with his students."

~Jack Nicklaus, World Golf Hall of Fame Member, 18 time Major Champion

---

"Like so many golfers at all levels of the game, Larry Rinker contracted the yips with his putter. Unlike many golfers, however, he conquered the malady, so much so that he wound up leading the PGA Tour in putting. I can't think of many achievements that are more inspiring, but inspiration is what Larry Rinker is all about. He truly is a Renaissance Man. Not only did he play, but he also moved in influential circles on the Player Advisory Council, and built a successful teaching practice. When he didn't have a golf club in his hands, he usually had a guitar, which he wielded with similar skill. Just ask Stephen Stills or Vince Gill or Darius Rucker, some of the many artists with whom he has played over the years. These days Larry spends most of his time teaching and he continues to shine. "The Journeyman" shows if you have a never-give-up attitude, you can accomplish anything. Congrats on the book, my friend."

~Brandel Chamblee, PGA Tour Winner, Golf Channel Analyst

"I've always held such high regard for those who not only have the talent, but dedication and fortitude to become members of the PGA Tour. The ultimate focus in any sport naturally gravitates to the star athletes, and the Tour has been blessed to have its share over the years. But for every high-profile performer, there are numerous others who are no less dedicated or focused, and have equally compelling stories to tell, but toil in comparative anonymity as they confront their personal challenges and disappointments, with the periodic triumph, all the while searching for those illusive mechanical and mental keys to sustained success.

This is why Larry Rinker's "The Journeyman" is not only enjoyable, but insightful in telling the "rest of the story" on the PGA Tour. To appreciate Larry's perseverance and relevance of this book's title, he is one of only four players

TESTIMONIALS

to have competed in more than 500 PGA Tour events without a win. That in itself covers a lot of heartbreak and success, self-doubt and confidence over the years.

Larry's personal story is certainly unique in its own right: coming from a highly accomplished golfing family (brother Lee played on the PGA Tour and sister Laurie on the LPGA), becoming an accomplished musician, reimagining his career several times over from player, to broadcaster/sports talk show host, to real estate agent, to acclaimed golf instructor. Now add author to the list. It's a story worth telling."

~ Tim Finchem, former commissioner, PGA Tour

"Larry is a rare combination of wonderful player, teacher and student. His insights into his own personal journey in these domains provide immense value not only to all golfers but to anyone who pursues excellence."

~ Fred Shoemaker, Author, "Extraordinary Golf," "Extraordinary Putting"

"Larry Rinker is a force of nature. He digs into everything he does with a world-class level of tenacity and commitment. Whether he's playing golf, broadcasting or playing through one of his favorite jazz standards on his custom, one-of-a-kind Fender Golfcaster guitar, it's always straight from the heart and world class. As host of Rinker's Golf Tips on satellite radio, he brings a unique combination of warmth, empathy and expertise to his interviews with the best golf teachers in the world. Several of my favorite shows have contained segments where Larry is flying solo, telling bits and pieces of his own life story. "The Journeyman" allows us all to learn the details of his accomplishments, struggles and travels, providing us with glimpses of his wisdom and spirit."

~ Rick Peckham, Guitar Professor, Berklee College of Music and Author of "Berklee Guitar Chords 101/201"

TESTIMONIALS

"I first met Larry in 1980 when we were both playing in the Florida Open at the Sinners course at Sandpiper Bay. On the par-five second hole he knocked it on in two, leaving himself a 20-foot putt. He proceeded to mark his ball with a silver dollar. I objected, noting that the rulebook says a ball marker must be a small object. He looked me right in the eye and said, "Define small." That's when I knew I was up against a lion. Larry and I became friends, and I couldn't be prouder of him for his accomplishments not only in golf, where he has succeeded as a player, teacher and broadcaster, but also in his personal life as a husband and father. Congratulations on this book, Larry. Best of luck and God bless."

~ *Bruce Fleisher, PGA Tour Winner, 18 Wins PGA Tour Champions*

"Larry Rinker has delivered a very interesting and personal glimpse of life and the challenges associated with competition at the highest level in the world – the PGA Tour. Born into one of the great families in golf, Larry has worked with many of the most innovative and progressive minds in the game, and the knowledge he gained, combined with his skill and creativity, produced a very successful career on Tour.

Our careers paralleled in many ways over the years. Larry became a trusted source of information and support for me as we both tried to challenge ourselves and constantly improve. "The Journeyman" should be an inspiration for those ready for a life of competition in pro golf or those just striving to be their best."

~ *Donnie Hammond, Two-Time winner on the PGA Tour*

"I've known the Rinker family – Larry, Lee and Laurie – for over 30 years. All three siblings are great Americans, great players and teachers, and, most important to me, great friends of mine.

Since he retired from playing the PGA Tour, Larry has become a world-class instructor. I love the concepts that Larry promotes and couldn't agree more with his philosophy. This book will help golfers of all handicaps, which is what makes Larry such an accomplished instructor. He keeps it simple! Kudos on "The Journeyman," my friend."

~ *Bob Ford, Seminole Golf Club*

TESTIMONIALS

"'The Journeyman' is a real look at PGA Tour life from the eyes of a crafty veteran. Larry takes me back to junior, college/amateur "JSN days" and on to the glorious and sometimes not so glorious life on Tour. To the lifelong friends made through our great game, supporters through the good times but most important through the tough times, too. Larry reminds me that besides Barbara Nicklaus, the best wives on Tour were all named Jan! Haas, Jacobsen, Clements, Rose, Cook and Rinker. All still going strong!"

~John Cook, 11-Time Winner on the PGA Tour

"I've known Larry Rinker for more than 30 years. Our friendship is rooted on the music side of his life. This book is filled with great stories of Larry's friendships and collaborations with some of the greatest and most celebrated musicians of our time. His journey as a golfer is even more compelling when reading about his struggles and triumphs in that fiercely competitive world. Larry writes about his life with great honesty, humility, humor, and the wisdom he has gained from life's roller-coaster ride. Along the way he found his "natural swing.""

~Steve Luciano, Freelance Guitarist/Teacher at Southeastern University

---

"Enjoy reading "The Journeyman," a story lived and told by Larry Rinker. It's a great read of Larry's life on and off the golf course. I've known Larry for over 35 years and it was a joy to go on his journey."

~Mark Wiebe, Two-time PGA Tour Winner and Five-time PGA Tour Champions Winner including 2013 Senior British Open

TESTIMONIALS

"It likely was inevitable that Larry Rinker and I would be drawn to each other – him a professional golfer with a passion for guitar and music, and me a professional drummer with a passion for golf. My most memorable golf experiences came while playing and hanging out with Larry during the time he played the PGA Tour. Conversely, Larry sat in playing guitar with my band Fourplay and we wrote a great song, "Green Augusta," that was aired on a CBS golf telecast . . . a proud moment for both of us. Having read a preview of Larry's soon-to-be released book, "The Journeyman," I look forward to what I know will be a great read."

- Harvey Mason, among the most recorded and in-demand drummers of all time, as well as a record producer and member of the band Fourplay.

"This book will give you an insight into the Rinker Family and Larry's journey through life. As Larry's older brother I have been blessed to be there from the very beginning. We started playing golf together and we also started playing guitar together. Larry excelled in both. He has a true love for golf and for music. He has had an incredible life using his gifts at both! I was blessed by Larry's music when he sang and played his guitar at my wife's Kellii's Celebration of Life Service in 2019. All who came knew Larry was a great golfer, and they found out he is a great musician too. I know you will enjoy reading this book about "The Journeyman," Larry Rinker!"

Laine Rinker Jr.

THIS BOOK IS DEDICATED IN LOVING MEMORY TO MY FATHER, LAINE RINKER. HE WAS THE PATRIARCH OF THE RINKER FAMILY, THE ONE WHO INSPIRED US TO CHASE OUR DREAMS AND NEVER GIVE UP.

The **Journeyman**
HOW A VETERAN TOUR PLAYER FOUND HIS SWING AFTER 50 YEARS

Larry Rinker

"Success is not final, failure is not fatal: it is the courage to continue that counts."
~ Winston Churchill

Edited by Alan Tays

© 2020 by Larry Rinker
ONE PUTT MUSIC PUBLISHING
The Journeyman, Copyright 2020, 9089675521
ISBN: 978-0-578-75304-1

Director of Instruction – The Ritz-Carlton Golf Club, Orlando, 2015-Present
Director of Instruction – Red Sky Golf Academy, Vail, Colorado, 2010-Present

RELEASE PUBLISHED 08/2020

Printed By–
Xerographic Digital Printing
407-490-0690
www.xerocopy.com

Design & Layout–
Blue Media Design
407-721-2583
www.bluemediadesign.com

TABLE OF CONTENT

Chapter 1
A Florida Flower Child 21

Chapter 2
Gator Tales and Mini-Tours 37
   Finding my game on the mini-tours 46

Chapter 3
PGA Tour Monday Qualifying 55

Chapter 4
Best Years 1984-1985 69
   1985: Best year 74
   TPC Stadium course 78

Chapter 5
Stephen Stills Tour – All Access 85

Chapter 6
Bob Rotella and Fender Music 97

Chapter 7
Dick Coop and Golf in the Kingdom 115
   1992. British Open, Muirfield 119

Chapter 8
John Daly's First Guitar 129

Chapter 9
On the Road Again, PGA Tour Style 139

Chapter 10
1999 and My Friend Payne Stewart 151

Chapter 11
Fred Shoemaker, Intention and Commitment 161

Chapter 12
Teaching Career Starts with Ty Tryon 179

Chapter 13
Short Game Guru-XM PGA Tour Radio 199

Chapter 14
Riomar, Red Sky and Rinker's Golf Tips 209

TABLE OF CONTENT

Chapter 15
Finding the Wright Balance...221
   Wright Balance 226
Epilogue..233

ACKNOWLEDGMENTS

Any author's expression of gratitude has to start with family, and mine sacrificed for me and supported me in ways I can never repay. So thank you to my parents, Laine and Pam Rinker; also my wife, Jan, and our three children: Devon, Trevor and Morgan. And of course my brothers Laine Jr. and Lee and my sister Laurie.

I'm proud to call myself a Florida Gator, and for that I thank my coach, Buster Bishop, who recruited me and gave me a full scholarship at a time when that was no longer the norm.

I became a professional golfer and later a golf teacher largely through the advice and support of one of the sport's legends, Bob Toski, who taught me to chase my dreams in both areas. For help with the mental side of the game I am indebted to my sports psychologists, Dr. Bob Rotella, Dr. Richard Coop and Fred Shoemaker.

As a teacher, I spent years trying to find my natural swing, which finally happened after Doc Wright created an amazing measuring system to help all golfers find their natural swing.

The Senior Tour, now known as PGA Tour Champions, is a wonderful opportunity for Touring pros to extend their playing careers beyond age 50. Steve Kropp was the one responsible for giving me a chance to compete on that circuit.

For my current positions as Director of Instruction at both Red Sky Golf Club in Vail, Colo., and The Ritz-Carlton Golf Club in Orlando, Fla., I am grateful to the people who hired me. That would be Jeff Hanson at Red Sky and Nathan Stith (who created the position for me) at The Ritz-Carlton.

One of the challenges of being a professional golfer is the repeated need to secure temporary accommodations at tournaments, seasonal jobs, etc. The other side of this coin, however, is the memorable people you meet along the way. For me, that group included Dick and Phyllis Dillon, with whom I stayed with in Vero Beach, and Pat Hamill, who has provided me a place to stay in Colorado. The three of them taught me the true meaning of hospitality.

ACKNOWLEDGMENTS

I never expected to become a radio broadcaster, but I am one, thanks to Chris Castleberry, who hired and trained me at XM PGA Tour Radio.

I would also like to thank the PGA Tour membership and staff along with Mike Skevington, Peter Kostis, Phil Ritson, David Leadbetter, Jim McLean, Robert Baker, Mitchell Spearman, John Elliott, Chuck Cook, Mac O'Grady, Dr. Bob Winters, Stan Utley, Sean Foley, James Leitz, David Orr, James Sieckmann, Dr. Rob Neal, Mike Adams, E.A. Tischler, Jon Sinclair, Dr. Sasho Mackenzie, Mark Cammarene, Bob Ford and Tracy Allen.

Also my guitar mentors: Joe Lindwurm, Stephen Stills, Steve Luciano, Vince Gill, Jimmy Stewart, Ray Benson, Dan Smith, Robben Ford and Rick Peckham.

Last but not least, producing this book would have been a much more daunting task without the substantial contributions of my editor, Alan Tays, and my good friend and technical guru, Rey Ortiz. And the book would have been much duller without the contributions of photographers Carl Alexander, Jules Alexander, Paul Lester, Leep Zelones, Reames Studio, Mike Ucciferro and Christian Rangel.

To all, I couldn't have done it without you.

Larry Rinker

FOREWORD

As Larry Rinker's golf instructor, I have had the privilege of teaching his entire family. I became very fond of his dad, who had a great interest in teaching golf. As for Larry, he had been to so many instructors that he almost created paralysis from analysis. Many professionals would have quit and found another vocation, but not Larry. His determination to succeed was amazing. He became a successful Tour player, a wonderful teacher, and a close friend.

Being a Tour player is a pressure-packed, lonely life. A player must have some kind of release to relieve the unrelenting pressure of playing well enough to keep his Tour card. Losing that card represents a loss of playing privileges and the constant threat of having to get a "real" job. Fortunately, Larry did have a release, a very effective one: music. He is an accomplished guitarist who has sat in with and earned the respect of many well-known artists, including his good friend Stephen Stills.

As Larry's playing career wound down, he made a smooth transition into teaching, where he has become one of the most respected figures in the business. Proof of that is the two Director of Instruction positions he holds at two of the country's most prestigious golf clubs: The Ritz-Carlton Golf Club in Orlando, Fla., and the Red Sky Golf Club in Vail, Colo. As a teacher, he shares many beliefs with me, including one very basic fundamental: You cannot standardize teaching, as all teachers communicate differently and all students learn differently.

"The Journeyman" is the most fascinating book I have ever read. I believe the reader will enjoy learning about his journey as much as he enjoyed making it.

Bob Toski,
Hall of Fame Teacher, 1954 PGA Tour Leading Money Winner

FOREWORD

Lots of people keep journals. Golfers do, certainly to keep up with the changes in their golf swings. Since college, Larry Rinker has probably kept three at a time. My friend "Rink," already gifted with a flytrap memory, has kept the most meticulous golf notes I've ever encountered. Unsparingly detailed and brutally honest, they form a masterful account from a keenly observant professional athlete, fully aware that his natural talent must be honed by decades of hard work.

Larry Rinker is a first-rate guitar player as well, disciplined and sensitive, with a refined touch and a professional's approach to music. As a poet, he seems very much aware of the need to step aside and let the words find him. Just don't forget to write them down.

An effective and dependable grooved golf swing can appear out of nowhere. The hard part is keeping it, particularly for a prodigy like Larry. Anyone who comes to the game before the age of 10 will notice that every few months, their swing doesn't work. So they run to the range and spend hours trying to fix it.

Eventually they will either be taught or realize for themselves that when they grow three inches, they have to adjust everything because they are bigger. Their pants didn't shrink. They just need new ones. And so begins the search for a new swing. For Larry, this has been a lifelong quest, one that triggers an even more profound search for self knowledge.

Whenever I hear the term "journeyman" applied to a professional athlete, I cringe at the faintly dismissive implication. Originally used to describe a highly trained, duly apprenticed craftsman, it has been misused regularly to imply some degree of mediocrity. Larry Rinker has put that myth to rest. In having intertwined all the elements of his search for self awareness, he has adroitly put the "journey" back in "journeyman" and made it a fitting title for this book. Well done, dear friend.

Stephen Stills,
The first person to be inducted twice on the same night into the Rock and Roll Hall of Fame for Buffalo Springfield, and Crosby, Stills and Nash.

FOREWORD

"The Journeyman" is a must read for any aspiring Tour player as well as anyone who is a fan of the PGA Tour. "These guys are good" for a reason.

When Larry was 6 years old, his lungs collapsed twice while he was having a kidney removed. Doctors gave him only a 50-50 chance of survival. He not only survived, he thrived, because he refused to be deterred by any obstacle that life put in his way. That determination is the foundation of Larry's success as a golf professional, a musician, a teacher and a radio personality.

Larry Rinker played on the PGA Tour for 20 years because he has no "give up." Larry is a fighter. You will see that from the first few pages to the end. There is a mental toughness about him that only great professionals have, no matter what the arena.

As you read this book, you will learn about his relationship with the late Payne Stewart; about taking John Daly to buy his first guitar; about the gigs Larry played with famous musicians, starting with Stephen Stills (of Crosby, Stills, Nash and Young) and about Larry's pursuit to "fix" his mind and his golf swing. His persistence to achieve perfection shines with the turn of every page. When he struggled, he sought out and learned from the mental Gurus of the '90s, from Dr. Bob Rotella to Dr. Richard Coop to Fred Shoemaker, and he shares his detailed notes from each.

Larry also shares the instruction that took him off the PGA Tour and into his next journeys toward becoming a teacher and a radio personality. As always, there were obstacles to surmount at every turn. And as always, he surmounted all of them.

This truly is a great read, and when you're done, perhaps you will get the feeling that I did – that Larry isn't done, not by a long shot.

David F. Wright,
Ph.D., PGA

INTRODUCTION

When the Covid-19 pandemic infiltrated the United States, it gave many of us the time to devote to something else. "You should write a book," my mom suggested. Actually, I already had a book in progress, which I started writing 20 years ago. I even had a title for it: "The Journeyman." I hadn't contributed to the draft in years, but now I had plenty of time to resume writing. I found legal pads and journals dating all the way back to my orientation for the PGA Tour in 1981.

I started playing golf at age 6 and started taking guitar lessons at the age of 8. One became my livelihood, the other my leisure pursuit. In golf, I met, befriended and competed with many of the game's best players, often holding my own. Likewise, in music I met, befriended and performed with some of the best players, again often holding my own (often to the amazement of friends who had thought my guitar playing was just a little hobby). Woven through this narrative of my journey are a lot of great memories, experiences and life lessons I learned along the way.

I always believed there was more than one way to swing a golf club. I saw it every week on the PGA Tour. I went down every possible path to find the right way for me, and many times I believed my swing wasn't working because it was all mental. Bob Rotella used to say there's a thousand things that work on the practice tee that don't work on the golf course. What works for one player might not work for another. It might have been a good fit for them, but it might not match up for me.

During my pursuit of becoming a better teacher, I finally found how my swing works. I also began to understand how other swings different from mine worked as well. I could now watch the great players from Sam Snead to Jack Nicklaus to Tiger Woods and see how their swings matched up for them. We are not all alike, so why should we believe we should all swing alike?

INTRODUCTION

I now understand the mechanics of my swing. It's simple fundamentals where my swing matches up now. I understand my misses and my swing feels freer and more natural. Now instead of playing golf swing, I get to go play golf and have fun being a creative shot maker. This book is the story of my journey to finding my golf swing, which involved some interesting side trips along the way.

Life has a funny way of twisting and turning. There were times in my golfing career when my back was against the wall and I somehow came through. There were also job opportunities that didn't come to fruition, but then there was something even better a little further down the road. You cannot connect the dots going forward. Only by looking back can we connect the dots and see how God was in control the whole time.

ALSO AVAILABLE

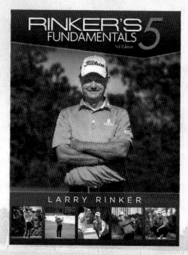

RINKER'S FUNDAMENTALS 5
3rd Edition

- Putting
- Short Game
- Distance Wedges
- Golf Swing
- Course Management

The Upper Core Swing
THE NEW REVOLUTION

- Determining Your Core Region
- Grip-Based on Carrying or Power Angle
- Set-up Characteristics of the Upper Core Swing
- Swing Characteristics
- Grip Size

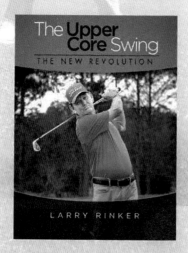

www.larryrinker.com

Chapter 1

A Florida Flower Child

A FLORIDA FLOWER CHILD

I was born in 1957 in Stuart, Fla., the second child of Laine and Pam Rinker. Although it's a small town, Stuart is the county seat of Martin County, which is just north of Palm Beach County on Florida's east coast.

My parents were from Bloomsburg, Pa., where my paternal grandfather, Franklin Rinker, had a wholesale flower business with his three sons. In 1954 F.O. Rinker and Sons expanded to Stuart. With the ability to grow flowers year-round, they could take advantage of the big holidays such as Valentine's Day, Christmas, Easter and Mother's Day.

Our house was small – it had only one bathroom and a combined living/dining room – but we had an acre of land right on the river. We were on a dirt road and rarely saw our neighbors, but we had several pets, including rabbits, German shepherds, a horse and a pony. The pony's name was Dolly and she tried to kill me a few times. She liked to gallop underneath the branches of the orange trees and try to knock me off. With my life flashing before my eyes, I would pull the reins with all my might, but she just kept going. One time when I was getting ready to mount her, she took off and my left foot got caught in the stirrup. The next thing I knew she was dragging me along the ground. Lucky for me the stirrup broke off and I didn't get trampled.

We were members of the First Baptist Church of Stuart, where my dad was a deacon and Sunday school director and my mom was involved with teaching Sunday school and singing in the choir. I literally cut my teeth there, and at the age of 7, I accepted Jesus Christ as my Lord and Savior.

Growing up in the country with only one TV in the house (which, in that pre-cable era, pulled in only three channels – ABC, NBC and CBS), we were forced to learn how to play together. And play we did. Everything we did was a competition, from cards to sports. Lee was the third child, three years younger than me, and Laurie was the baby, two years younger than Lee. With hardly any neighbors nearby, Lee and I usually played against my oldest brother Laine Jr. and Laurie. One day while playing flag football I realized I couldn't get to Laurie's flag, so I tripped her just before the goal line. Unfortunately, the goal line was our concrete driveway and Laurie broke her leg.

Laine Jr. was kind of a jack of all trades and would go on to play junior-college golf, first at Brevard Community College and then at Indian River Community College in Fort Pierce. After two quarters at the University of Florida he came home to help Mom run the farm. He would later graduate from Cal State Fullerton.

Our family was great at sarcastic humor, and Lee, unfortunately, was an easy target. He had quite the temper, and didn't like to take grief from anyone, even if it was Lee joking around, saying, "Wait till I get my temper up." Lee would launch his tirades – on separate occasions he hit me in the head with a toy gun and a 3-wood – and sometimes he'd even hurt himself. Lee put his hand not once, but twice through the window in the garage when we wouldn't let him in to play Ping-Pong.

A FLORIDA FLOWER CHILD

Laurie was your basic tomboy. With three older brothers, she had to be. She played all sports but was especially good at golf. She once won a junior tournament by 73 shots! Laurie won many junior titles, including the 1980 U.S. Girls' Junior Championship.

Golf was in our genes. Dad had taken up the game at age 26 and became good enough to win the club championship at Martin County Country Club. He also discovered that a great way to baby-sit the kids was to take them to the golf course. One day when I was 6, Laine Jr. came home from a junior clinic and said, "Hey, there's a kid that's 6 out here and you should come to the clinic." I did and before I knew it, golf was becoming a big part of my life. My dad was able to buy me a yearly membership at Martin County Country Club for only $15!

Being the son of a flower farmer made me – literally – a flower child. However, that lifestyle wasn't always easy. You could be awoken at 7 a.m. on a Saturday when extra hands were needed to get the work done. This could be anything from packing flowers to pulling a hose (my least favorite job) to bunching the flowers in the field. We all worked for minimum wage, which was under $2 an hour for most of our childhoods. When Dad gave us the choice to work on the farm this summer or work on your golf game, the decision was easy.

During 1963 and '64, I was hospitalized twice. On the second occasion, my left kidney was removed. I remember being wheeled into the operating room at St. Mary's Hospital in West Palm Beach and falling asleep from the anesthesia.

THE JOURNEYMAN

Right after I came out of the surgery, my lungs collapsed. My mother later told me what she had told the doctor: "He can't go back into surgery after what he's been through." There was no choice, though. "Mrs. Rinker," the doctor said, "do you want your son to live? He has about a 50/50 chance if we go in right now." So they went back in and stabilized my lungs.

I couldn't eat anything for days afterward. My lungs collapsed again and all I remember is being hooked up to a lung machine and occasionally getting to suck on some ice. It was a very lonely time for me because my parents couldn't visit often with St. Mary's being an hour's drive from home. But my mom came and saw me every day and that meant more to me than she'll ever know.

When I finally got home from the hospital I couldn't go to school, and I was way behind. I missed six to eight weeks of the first grade but thanks to my teacher and family I was able to pass. Contact sports were out. I got to play at home with my brothers and sister but at school it was a no-go because of the liability. Thankfully, I was able to play baseball and golf.

One day after my surgery I remember my dad bringing home a red plaid bag with seven clubs in it. Driver, 3-wood, 3-iron, 5-iron, 7-iron, 9-iron and putter. I don't recall what brand they were, but it was my first set and my dad had a huge smile on his face when he gave them to me. In baseball, I was a left-handed pitcher but I batted right-handed, so these golf clubs were right-handed. In those days getting a decent set of left-handed clubs was next to impossible. To this day, the only two things I do right-handed are play golf and play guitar.

A FLORIDA FLOWER CHILD

There was only one golf course in Martin County, the Martin County Country Club. This is where I hit my first ball, played my first round, made my first birdie, and won the club championship. In the junior clinics the pro had an old tire out on the range, and he told us to swing and hit the tire with our clubhead. I didn't know it at the time, but it was one of the greatest lessons I ever had. Today, people make a lot of money selling impact bags that accomplish the same thing.

Spending entire days at the golf course, we came up with all sorts of games to play. One of our favorites was stymies, where you had to try to make a putt despite another player's ball being in the way. Lee and I also made holes in the backyard at home and would play for hours. We had our own course along the river through the Australian Pines.

Besides sports, my other love was music. For Christmas in 1964 my grandparents got Laine Jr. and me the first two Beatles albums. We wore those two records out. I would accompany the music by pretending to play a Mickey Mouse guitar we had gotten from every kid's favorite reading material of that era – the Sears, Roebuck catalog. Laine and I even had Beatle wigs, which really set us apart from other boys our ages, almost all of whom had crewcuts. I was starting to sing in the choir at church and I even sang a duet with a girl in front of the whole elementary school.

In third grade I started taking guitar lessons, and in fourth grade I got my first electric guitar – a Kent Guyatone Americana – and a Fender Deluxe Reverb amp. My teacher through high school was Joe Lindwurm, a trumpet player from New York. Guitar was his second instrument. He taught me how to read music. As I progressed, our lessons eventually took the form of me playing rhythm guitar while he played his trumpet. Joe used to tell me to quit messing with golf because I could make more money playing music.

1965: Larry

In sixth grade I was in my first band. We called ourselves "The Realms of Paradise." We played for two nights in front of about 2,000 people in a charity function at the Martin County High School gym. This was so long ago that we plugged our microphones into the same amps as our guitars. If that doesn't mean anything to you, trust me, it's not something someone would do today.

Through sixth grade baseball was my main sport in the summertime. In my last year of little league we won the county championship and beat the all-stars! I was a pitcher and remember the more I concentrated on the catcher's mitt, the better I pitched. Later on, I would apply this to golf with great results. Get into the target and see the ball going there. My golf game was also improving, and I had to choose between playing baseball or the Florida junior golf circuit.

I opted for golf. My first tournament outside of Martin County was the Crutchfield Junior in Sebring, Fla. I was 11 playing in the 12-and-under age division. We played nine holes each day. On the first day I was paired with someone who would become a good friend, David Abell. David was 8, the son of a junior-college golf coach. By age 14 he was the best junior player on the planet and would go on to win the Arnold Palmer Scholarship to Wake Forest. His path would veer away from professional tournament golf and he would become the business manager and partner of multiple major champion Nick Price.

As I said, Abell and I became good friends. We've played a lot of golf together over the years, and though he certainly won his share of our matches, he recently paid me a touching compliment. When he learned I was writing this book and he would be a part of it, he texted me this message (and gave me permission to use it in the book):

> "I hope ur writing about kicking my ass across the saints and sinners for 10 years which lead you to the PGA Tour and sent me packing overseas in shame for 20 years!!!"

Now, back to that tournament in Sebring:
After a nervous night, highway noise and my father's snoring prevented me from getting much sleep. I shot 51 for my nine-hole first round, with David Abell shooting a similar score.

THE JOURNEYMAN

I was shocked, however, to see that some kid from Fort Lauderdale named Buddy Rountree had shot 37. My best score at age 11 was an 87. Buddy followed his 37 with a 38 and won the tournament. I shot another score in the 50s and had my first real taste of tournament golf.

For Christmas in 1968 Santa Claus brought me a whole new set of clubs: 1-3-4-5 woods, 3-4-5-6-7-8-9-PW-SW, and a new bag and headcovers. Wow! That summer, 1969, I played in the big Florida junior tournaments for the first time, including the State Jaycees, State Junior and State PGA Junior. In the Crutchfield Junior I finished second. I broke 80 for the first time that summer, shooting a 79 in a practice round.

As you can imagine, the competition in the Florida junior ranks was fierce. But the Rinkers were holding their own. In his first tournament, Lee beat future PGA Tour player Steve Hart (who was a year older) in a playoff. Future British Open champion Mark Calcavecchia was playing against Lee and Steve as well.

Larry, Lee and Laurie at the 1972 PGA State Junior in Wildwood, Fla.

A FLORIDA FLOWER CHILD

The early 1970s saw me experiencing the pressure of leading a tournament for the first time. In 1972 in a state tournament at Wildwood, Fla., I slept on my first lead in the 14-15 age group of the PGA Junior. The next day I tried to hit a 1-iron out of the trees on No. 8, made a triple bogey and shot 80. I still made it to a playoff, but I bogeyed the first hole and lost. Laurie and Lee won their respective age divisions.

In the early 1970s I got a job at Holiday Country Club in Stuart picking the range and parking carts. It was here that I met a PGA teacher named Mike Skevington in 1972. He taught me how to chart a course for yardages and he also helped me figure out how far I hit each club. We didn't have lasers or yardage wheels, so I just walked my normal stride, counting each step as a yard. The first tournament I played in with my new system was the Crutchfield Junior. I played well and finished second to Mike Donald of Hollywood. Mike would go on to win once on the PGA Tour but is best known for dueling Hale Irwin through an 18-hole playoff in the 1990 U.S. Open at Medinah before falling on the first hole of sudden death.

My distance-measuring system continued to work in my next event as I recorded my first score in the 60s – a 69 in the first round at Delray Dunes. I wound up finishing second, and Lee won his age division again.

Life was great. I was working at a golf course just a mile from home and we were also members at Sandpiper Bay and Martin County Country Club. Before I was old enough to drive, I would take our boat "Ma Petite" up to Sandpiper Bay. It was a 14-foot boat with an Evinrude 25 motor on the back. The marina was only a short walk from the pro shop at the Sinners course at Sandpiper.

Golf was the family sport, thanks to Dad. He was the one who gave us the inspiration to pursue the game. He carried a 1-handicap and was the club champion and chairman of the greens committee. He had an old gas cart that he kept at the home of one of his best friends, Dr. Allison, about a half-mile from Martin County CC. With no governor on the engine and a winding road to traverse, we had some pretty scary rides to the golf course. Fortunately, we never had an accident.

1972: The Rinker family: Laine and Pam, with sons Laine Jr., Larry and Lee and daughter Laurie

In the summer of 1974, I finally won a big event, the State Jaycees at Lehigh Acres, closing with a 66. Dad was there, and we had a great trip home. I remember he had been stung by a bee that day, but he didn't let it spoil the fun on our ride home. That was just another example of the sacrifices my parents made so that we could play tournaments in the summertime.

In the fall, Laine Jr. and I went down to Miami with our guitar teacher, Joe Lindwurm, to purchase guitars at ACE Music. I had never been in a music store that large before. Laine bought a Martin D-28 and I got a Gibson SG. I really wanted a Les Paul but I went with the less expensive SG. We finally had some "real" guitars!

In my senior year of high school, I was picking the range at the Sinners course at Sandpiper Bay when I met a guy from my speech class who played guitar well. He was into Deep Purple, Jimi Hendrix and David Bowie. I was into the Doobie Brothers, Eagles, America, Bachman Turner Overdrive and Crosby, Stills, Nash and Young. We ended up playing only three gigs, but we practiced a lot and had a lot of fun. I was also starting to surf, and I wasn't spending much time on my golf game.

There was a big tournament during Christmas break in Miami called the International Junior Orange Bowl. My instructor wasn't too happy with all my extracurricular activities and told me I didn't deserve to play well in Miami. I finished second to my old friend David Abell, who won the tournament by eight shots and was only 15. There were a few players who played that year who went on to win tournaments on the PGA Tour, including Gary Hallberg, John Cook and Nick Price.

Over the next few months I visited three schools on recruiting trips: Florida, Florida State and Texas A&M. Texas A&M's coach, Bob

Ellis, used to live in Stuart and I was invited to go check out the campus. I really wanted to go to Florida because they had the best team. The only question was about a scholarship. Florida hadn't offered anything yet and Florida State and Texas A&M had.

I let Florida's coach, Buster Bishop, know that I wanted to go to Florida. He called one day in the spring of 1975 and said he wanted to come down and sign me to a scholarship. That's it. Scholarship. I thought, "How much?" The coach is driving four hours each way down to see me and I don't know how much the scholarship is for. One quarter? One half? Three quarters? Full? I asked my dad if I still could go to Florida even if I didn't get a full scholarship. He said yes, so now the only suspense was "How much is the scholarship for?" So, when Coach Bishop arrived, there was my family, Mike Skevington and a reporter from the Stuart News, and we were all dying to know the answer. As I was signing the letter of intent, I asked the coach what kind of scholarship it was. "Full," he said, "including books and everything!" My parents breathed a sigh of relief, and it meant a lot to me to know that the coach thought that much of me. Getting a full ride at this time was flattering, because full scholarships for golf were being reduced from eight to five, and a lot of coaches were splitting up the scholarships and giving halves.

After signing with Florida, I made a few trips to Gainesville before I graduated from high school. On the first trip I got to stay with future Tour player Andy Bean. There was a field near the agricultural department that the team would sometimes hit balls at, known as Hidden Field. Bean's roommate, George Graefe, had decided one day while he was hitting balls that he wanted to get a tan all over. The only problem was the University Police used to like to eat their lunch nearby and one of them caught George in his birthday suit with just his glove and Foot-Joys on. The field was renamed "Naked Field."

That summer I played in some major amateur tournaments for the first time. I was the medalist at the Western Junior and lost in the quarterfinals. Being medalist earned me an invitation to the Western Amateur. I finished 10th at the Southern Amateur and played with Curtis Strange in the third round. Curtis was a stud from Wake Forest and was one of the best amateurs on the planet. I also set two course records. I was playing the best golf of my life and was ready to go to Gainesville and start college.

Chapter 2

Gator Tales and Mini-Tours

GATOR TALES AND MINI TOURS

Larry was Medalist in the 1975 Western Junior in Stillwater, Okla.

At the University of Florida if you were on scholarship you had to live in the athletic dorm your first year. Yon Hall was in the east side of Florida Field and a great location for the football games. The Gators hadn't yet climbed to the heights they would reach in later years – winning national championships in 1996, 2006 and 2008. But they almost always had winning records and were extremely tough to beat in "The Swamp," their home field. In four years I hardly missed a home game.

Being on scholarship allowed me to park on campus just south of the south end zone. I also got to eat at the training table for the athletes. During football season we got steak twice a week. I gained 10 pounds the first quarter!

THE JOURNEYMAN

Each year at Florida, Coach Bishop would have open tryouts for the golf team. Anybody could walk on. At our first team meeting, more than 100 guys showed up. We had to play eight rounds in the first few weeks and the rounds counted if we played with another team member.

Coach liked to keep a lot of freshmen. About half of the 40 guys on our team were freshmen. You never knew if one of these freshmen might blossom into a great player. Several years earlier Bob Murphy went to Florida on a baseball scholarship but got hurt in his freshman year. He started playing golf with the team and ended up winning the U.S. Amateur in his junior year. He went on to have a distinguished pro career, winning several times on the PGA and Senior Tours.

The first tournament of my freshman year was the Tucker Invitational in Albuquerque, N.M. This was a big event, and the course was also the host course for the NCAA tournament in May. I got to go, but it wasn't the start that I had hoped for. After playing poorly the first round I asked Coach to come watch me play the front nine the next day. After six three-putts on the front nine, Coach had seen enough. The greens were about 10,000 square feet and the fastest things I had ever seen. I ended up shooting 40 over par for the four rounds.

The next tournament was the Florida Intercollegiate at my home course, the Sinners at Sandpiper Bay. I played well the first two rounds but on the last day I shot 86. Our team won but I didn't feel like a winner.

GATOR TALES AND MINI TOURS

The rest of my freshman year was about as uneventful as the first two tournaments, but Coach kept playing me. Some other guys on the team should have been going to the tournaments but my name kept appearing on the list. The list. We didn't have qualifying at Florida. Coach felt that the tournaments were the best place to test the players rather than head-to-head battles back at the home track. For each tournament a list would be posted with the names of those who would get to play. Some of the choices didn't sit too well with some of the players and I didn't blame them.

The summer between my freshman and sophomore years would end up being a turning point in my career. My dad arranged for me to go see Bob Toski in Miami. Toski, a fine player in his day who became a highly regarded instructor, taught me that if I got my left arm through impact, I could turn it over as hard as I wanted to with my arms and hands, and not hit it left. I couldn't believe it. I kept looking up, expecting to see the ball going left, but it was just gently drawing, right to left, right at the flagstick. The next tournament I played in was the Southern Amateur at Colonial Country Club in Memphis. I hit it great, but I was starting to get the yips. Yeah, the yips with the putter.

When Laine Jr. went to the University of Florida in 1974, he lived in an apartment, and then purchased a trailer. I asked my dad if we could move the trailer to the Windmeadows trailer park and we did. I would live in it for three years and then Laurie would live there later as well. My first roommate was Sam Trahan, and then Rick Pearson. While I was living there it really irritated me when

THE JOURNEYMAN

Jimmy Buffett came out with a song that ended with:

> *I'm just a son of a son, son of a son*
> *Son of a son of a sailor*
> *The sea's in my veins, my tradition remains*
> *I'm just glad I don't live in a trailer*

My dad now arranged for me to go see Andy Bean's dad in Lakeland for some putting tips. Andy was a great putter and his dad was his coach. He helped me a lot but when I went to qualify for the U.S. Amateur, the yips showed up again. My sophomore year was my worst year. I got to play with the A team just twice. I had work to do.

I knew there was hardly any chance I could make putts while flinching. To conquer the yips, I had to change my perception of success. Success no longer was the ball going in the hole, but rather a smooth stroke and the ball rolling nicely. On the 10th hole at the State Amateur at Bay Hill, I had a 40-footer for birdie. It rolled five feet past. I made a smooth stroke and the ball rolled nicely, right over the right edge of the cup about five inches past. Despite the missed putt for par I told myself, "I'm getting better." I would later learn that these are process goals – things you can do on every shot no matter the outcome. At the Rice Planters tournament, I turned the corner with my putting and then I won a tournament in Lake City, Fla., right before school started. I was back.

In qualifying my junior year, I played well and finished second. I could not believe it when my name was not on the list for the first tournament. When I asked Coach why he said, "You're not ready yet." I was so mad that I went out and shot 29 on the front nine with a hole-in-one on No. 2 and a bogey-6 on No. 7. After shooting 7 under par on the front, I didn't even play the back nine.

I finally got to play in the tournament at Grenelefe, which was a very hard course. I had the second-best score on our team. That was the only tournament I played in that fall. When someone asked our assistant coach how the team was doing, he said, "We did well here and there and tried out some guys at Grenelefe." Yeah, I guess I was still a tryout, but I knew I was playing some of the best golf on the team.

In the winter quarter at Florida we had our Orange and Blue practices. Every Saturday and Sunday we played a shotgun start at 7 a.m. no matter how cold it was. Some mornings it was in the 20s. One week, in my junior year, Mark Calcavecchia came on a recruiting trip and wanted to play with the team in the Orange and Blues. He played well the first day, but Sunday morning was really cold. He wasn't playing well and on No. 17 he skulled his second shot over the green and said, "I'm never coming back to this place again." Calc ended up coming to Florida the next fall.

Coach said that whoever finished first and second in the Orange and Blues for all the weeks preceding the inaugural Gator Invitational would get to play. I finished second in the qualifying, then shot 70 the last day of the tournament to finish T-10 to help our team finish second in the first Gator Invitational. I was back in the starting lineup.

I had some other good finishes in the spring. The last tournament before the NCAA Championship was the SEC Championship at newly opened Shoal Creek in Birmingham, Alabama. I was playing well in the second round, but I double-bogeyed 18 to shoot 74. That left me just four shots back going into the final round. The course was playing so tough that 4 over was leading. Georgia, with future PGA Tour player Chip Beck (who opened with 82-72), had a 22-shot lead on us going into the final round.

Larry, the 1978 SEC Individual champion, posing in front of the trailer

My goal in the final round was to play well enough to finish in the top 5 and earn all-conference honors. The wind was gusting 30-40 mph, but going into 18 I was 2 under for the day. I missed the green and chipped to about five feet. I was so nervous over that putt that I didn't have any idea how I was going to get it in. Somehow, I just hit it on a jerk and got it in for par to shoot 70–222, 6 over par. Georgia was still out on the golf course, but just before we flew back home we learned that Georgia had beaten us by only three shots. Individually, I had just won the SEC by two shots over Chip Beck and Bill Britton. Wow! SEC Champ!

In my senior year our team was deep. We had the Anton twins, junior college transfers Rick Pearson and Ken Green, Pat Venker, Mark Calcavecchia, Tony Deluca, Jim Prim, Larry Rentz and a lot of other good players. We won six tournaments during the season and going into the SEC we were brimming with confidence.

The 1979 Gator golf team: From L to R standing, Terry Anton, Larry, Coach Bishop, John Darr. Kneeling, Rick Pearson, Ken Green, Pat Venker

At the SEC Championship we didn't play too well. During the last round something caused our assistant coach, John Darr, to think that Rick Pearson had become angry and quit trying because he appeared to not walk off a yardage on one hole. Darr decided that

Rick would not be going to the NCAAs, and he replaced Rick with Tom Anton. This was devastating to the team. We were a little dysfunctional at the NCAAs and barely made the cut, ultimately finishing tied for 15th. Ohio State won the championship with John Cook, Marc Balen, Rob Brewster and Joey Sindelar.

After the last round of the NCAA Championship, Wally Uihlein, who at the time was the national sales manager for Titleist, approached me. "I hear you are turning professional," he said. "We'd like to provide you with balls, hats and gloves." That started a long friendship. Wally would later become the president and CEO of Titleist and Foot-Joy Worldwide. My college career was over. I graduated with honors in June with a degree in Finance and won the Doug Beldon award for the most outstanding graduating athlete.

I was ready to turn pro.

Finding my game on the mini-tours

The week after the State Amateur I turned pro and went with my brother Lee to work with Bob Toski in Boca Raton, Florida. Toski was this sharp-witted little bantamweight – at 5-feet-7, 118 pounds, he had been the smallest player on the PGA Tour – who had been the circuit's leading money winner in 1954. Despite that success, he left the Tour two years later at age 30, to go into teaching and help raise his family.

Toski's $65,820 Tour-leading total was misleading; it included $50,000 for winning the second World Championship of Golf. He also got another $50,000 in unofficial money to do 50 exhibitions for the following year. In 1954 Sam Snead beat Ben Hogan in a playoff at the Masters to win $5,000. Ed Furgol took home $6,000 for winning the U.S. Open. Toski winning the World Championship of Golf is akin to 2019, when Rory McIlroy won $15 million winning the FedEx Cup and Tiger Woods and Gary Woodland won just over $2 million for the Masters and U.S. Open.

Toski became a teaching legend. He pioneered the Golf Digest Schools with Jim Flick, Peter Kostis, Davis Love Jr., John Jacobs, Paul Runyan, Bob Rotella, Chuck Cook, John Elliott and others. Bob was the first inductee in the World Golf Teachers Hall of Fame who was still alive at the time of his induction.

Toski treated Lee and me like kings. He refused to let us pay for anything. For three days straight he worked and played golf with us every day. We would work on the range from 9 a.m. to noon, then have lunch and go play a great golf course in the afternoon.

I played in more than 10 events to get ready for the Tour's qualifying tournament – better known as Q-School – in the fall. My second event was the Florida Open at my home course, Sandpiper Bay. I noticed that the things I worked on with Toski for my swing were working great, but I had come down with the yips with the putter again. I finally started looking at the hole so I wouldn't flinch and would have a chance to make some putts. Somehow, I finished T-10.

When you are playing the mini-tours, anytime you could save a dollar by staying with someone or traveling together with another player, you did. My parents had given me $2,200 for graduation, and I wanted to stretch that bankroll as far as I could. In Pinehurst, a college teammate of Lee's, Kelly Miller, had married one of the Bell girls, whose parents owned Pine Needles. The parents were Warren "Bullet" Bell and his wife Peggy Kirk Bell, the famous LPGA golfer-turned teacher. I had a place to stay with one of their assistant pros for the month, and anytime I wanted to play and practice at Pine Needles, I could.

Some of the most competitive golf on the mini-tours is played in the practice rounds. The day before the first round at Whispering Pines, a guy named Mitch Kemper came up to me and asked if he could join me in a practice round. I agreed, we played 18 holes and then I suggested we go play Pine Needles. There on the first tee were two other pros who were looking for a game. Mitch and I said yes, then proceeded to get our brains beat in. On the 17th hole Mitch asked me, "Who are these guys?" "The first guy is Scott Hoch, an All-American from Wake Forest University," I said, "and the other guy is Gary Trivisonno, who played No. 1 at Alabama."

I made a few small checks, but I failed to advance out of the first stage at Q-School. Now I was broke. I asked my dad if I could borrow $2,000 to play five events on the Space Coast mini-tour in Orlando. The deal was, if I lost that, I would get a job and pay Dad back. Fortunately, I finished second in the third tournament, paid Dad back and had enough money to put up the $2,000 for the next series.

Going into the final tournament before Christmas in 1979, I needed to make a check to pay for the next series in 1980. I thought I could go back to my dad and get another $2,000, but this time he said no. "It would do your ass good to go to work!" he said. My dad was tough on me. I somehow finished second in that last tournament and had enough money to buy a new $500 Ovation acoustic guitar and pay for the next series.

1980 ended up being quite a year for me. In March I open-qualified for my first PGA Tour event, the Bay Hill Classic in Orlando. I missed the cut, but gained valuable experience. In the spring at Q-School I missed again at first stage but qualified for the U.S. Open at Baltusrol in New Jersey. Lee came up and caddied for me. I missed the cut again, but I learned that when you have a short iron in your hands. you better take advantage of that opportunity.

On the way home from the Open I stopped at Hilton Head to see a guy who was interested in sponsoring me. He agreed to put up half of the money I needed, and we would split what I made.

In 1980, Space Coast mini-tour owner and operator J.C. Goosie decided to add a summer series to his product: 12 events in all, divided into three four-tournament series. I signed up to play, with the goal of getting a win. My new sponsor had talked to me about playing the game shot by shot and staying in the present. My dad had always said if I could shoot in the 60s two days in a row, I could win. I hadn't done it yet, but in the first tournament I shot in the 60s both days and finished second! The next tournament I won.

By the end of the summer I had won three of the 12 tournaments and was leading money winner. There was a new mini-tour going on in Cape Cod in Massachusetts in September. I met my buddy, Mitch Kemper, in New York before we headed to the Cape. Mitch was quite a singer/musician and we went to see Mel Torme perform at Marty's. I had never heard such a pure voice. I was starting to listen to Frank Sinatra, George Benson and Michael Franks. The commercial jazz scene was just starting to take off.

At the Cape I continued to play well, won two out of six tournaments and was leading money winner again. Mitch and I went and watched our coach, Bob Toski, play in the Commemorative Tournament in Rhode Island. The Senior Tour had just started the year before at the Legends of Golf in Austin, Texas.

We also got a chance to see my friend, Wally Uihlein, at the Titleist factory in New Bedford, Massachusetts. He gave us a private tour of the factory and it was cool to see how a golf ball was made. It was a great summer and now it was time for Q-School in the fall.

I finally made it to the finals of Q-School, which in 1980 was played in Fresno, Calif. My older brother, Laine Jr., caddied for me. The first round I shot 78 with 39 putts. How was I going to qualify if I couldn't putt? I made a five-footer for par on the first hole of the second round, but ended up missing my card by one shot with a score of 287. Mark O'Meara and Fred Couples made that school. Qualifying for the Tour was now not just a fantasy. If I could shoot 78 the first round and miss by only a shot, I could make it. There was no Hogan/Nike/Korn Ferry Tour then, so it was back to the mini-tours in Florida.

I won the first tournament back on the Space Coast mini-tour and Golfweek magazine named me mini-tour player of the year for 1980. For the year, I had won six tournaments and about $60,000 in prize money.

GATOR TALES AND MINI TOURS

In the fall of 1980 I played in a tournament unlike any other I had ever experienced. Officially called the Doyle Brunson World Match Play Championship, it was better known as the "Texas Dolly," which was Brunson's nickname. Brunson was the top poker player of the era, and a golf nut as well. The event he put together had a $5,000 entry fee, but whoever survived five rounds of match play would collect $50,000. That was only $5,000 less than the winners of the Masters and U.S. Open were paid. And unlike those tournaments, the Dolly paid out in cash!

Deane Beman sent out a letter to all PGA Tour members reminding them that associating with gamblers was forbidden, so that left all the mini-tour players and club pros to make up the 32-player field. A friend of mine, Gary Sorensen, agreed to sponsor me, and Mitch came to caddie.

I had never been to Las Vegas. We were staying at the Dunes Hotel and playing their golf course. The Bellagio Hotel now sits on this property. I lost my first match, so I went into the consolation bracket with the other 15 losers. Whoever could win the next four matches would get $7,500. My first consolation match was against Steve Bull from Milwaukee, the same town Gary Sorensen was from. A bunch of guys from Milwaukee had decided to sponsor Steve and go have some fun in Las Vegas. The funny thing was that Gary hadn't told any of them until they got out there that he was sponsoring me, too.

On the ninth green of our match after I three-putted, Steve Bull said to me, "Hey, cut that crap out, kid. I got a plane to catch at 3." I ended up winning the match and the rest of the matches, so we ended up paying for our little trip to Las Vegas. The best part was that I got to stay all week, saw some great shows, which included Tony Bennett, and got to be buddies with Mark Wiebe.

Sometime just before Christmas, I received an invitation out of the blue to play in the 1981 Bing Crosby National Pro-Am at Pebble Beach. Bing's son Nathaniel Crosby was good friends with Mickey Van Gerbig, an attorney and fine player from Palm Beach, who represented Ben Crenshaw. Mickey invited Nathaniel to play with him in the International four-ball in Miami that Mickey hosted. That's where I met Nathaniel and we became friends. I couldn't believe it. Pebble Beach! I had never been there.

It cost me about $1,500 to go to the Crosby, and I didn't play very well, mostly because of poor putting. I went back to Florida and tried to open-qualify for the Doral event in Miami and the Jackie Gleason Inverrary Classic, west of Fort Lauderdale. I made the qualifier for Inverrary but missed the cut again with poor putting. Mitch was caddying for me and when my dad came up to him to give me some technical advice Mitch said, "He's choking his guts out, Mr. Rinker!"

A few months later one of my neighbors knocked on my door holding a Golf Journal and asked, "What is your last name?" When I replied, "Rinker," he said, "It says here that you have hit the longest drive on the PGA Tour this year!" He kept looking up and down at my 5-foot-8 frame and couldn't believe this 150-pound guy could hit the ball so far. I was considered sneaky long in those days and I had no idea that I even hit the longest drive that day at Inverrary.

GATOR TALES AND MINI TOURS

One thing about traveling and trying to open-qualify: You don't make any money unless you can qualify and make the cut. So far in 1981 I had made hardly any money, and it is a lot more expensive to travel and play than it is to play out of a home base in Orlando on the mini-tours.

The first stage of Q-School was at the Magnolia course at Disney World in Lake Buena Vista, Fla., a course I knew well. I was leading going into the last round and I remember telling myself that if I could win this stage, I was ready to qualify for the Tour. I won. The finals were at the Palm course at Disney World.

I played practice rounds with Payne Stewart and Mark Wiebe. Mitch had told me about this guy from Missouri who could really play and who was someone I needed to meet. Payne had undergone acupuncture and part of the needles were still stuck in his ears. He had a bag tag that read "Think" on one side and "Tempo" on the other. We had a great time playing the dot game. You would get a dot for: longest drive, fairway, first on the green, closest to the pin, inside the length of the flagstick, inside the leather, birdie, sandy, low ball and green in regulation. You could get 8 or 9 points on a par-five. We played a dollar a point and gave each other grief the whole time.

After three rounds, I was in the top 25, which is where you had to be to earn your Tour card. In the final round on the first hole, I blocked my tee shot and laid up in the bunker on the par-five. I ended up having a five-footer for par and somehow got it in. That relaxed me a little, but I was nervous nevertheless. I birdied 15 to get in a position where I could bogey the last three holes and make it. I parred 16 and bogeyed 17 and 18 to make it by a shot. On 18 I played very conservatively. No time to make a stupid mistake. I was in! PGA Tour here we come! I qualified with Payne Stewart, Denis Watson, Mark Calcavecchia and Clarence Rose. I remember asking Payne how he played and he said, "I shot 69, hit 16 greens and hit it good!!" He was beaming with confidence.

Chapter 3

PGA Tour Monday Qualifying

PGA TOUR MONDAY QUALIFYING

In 1981 only the top 60 money winners from the previous year and current winners, guys who had won tournaments in the last calendar year, were exempt from qualifying to play in events on the PGA Tour. The rest of the membership had to Monday-qualify. Most of the 18-hole qualifiers were held on the tournament course, but this wasn't always the case. These were different than the open qualifiers that I had played in previously.

The players eligible to play in the Monday-qualifiers were:

1. The top 61-160 money winners from the previous year
2. Q-School graduates
3. Any previous winner on the PGA Tour
4. Club pros who had acquired a Class A membership to the PGA of America (one-year access)

To keep your card as a rookie you had to win a minimum of $2,000 less than 160th on the money list the previous year. For my rookie class, that meant we had to win $10,500 to keep our cards. That's pocket change on today's Tour, where 160th on the 2018-19 money list – hello, Hudson Swafford – earned $545,191.

We had other sources of income, too. Unofficial ones, which didn't count on the money list but spent just the same. The stars, of course, had endorsement contracts that paid them for having sponsors' logos on their bags, shirts and hats. But the rest of us had money-making opportunities, too.

THE JOURNEYMAN

My sponsor was Titleist, which had weekly pools for those of us who played the ball. It was always great to see the PGA Tour representative for Titleist, Joe Turnesa Jr., after you had played well. You couldn't miss his snow-white Titleist blazer, and you knew he was carrying envelopes with bonus checks just for you.

In 1981 a lot of guys drove from Tour stop to Tour stop. The schedule was set up so that you could play several tournaments in a region of the country. The West Coast swing and the Florida swing were examples. The tough part was if you didn't qualify, what did you do for a week until the next tournament? You found a place to stay and practice. And if you made the cut you had to go play the next week because you were in the tournament. This made the 36-hole cut very important for non-exempt players otherwise known as "rabbits."

In June I packed up my 1979 Camaro, traveling with Mitch Kemper as my caddie, and we headed up for my first tournament, the St. Jude Classic in Memphis. Mitch introduced me to jazz, and I finally started appreciating the standards and the vocal work of Frank Sinatra and other jazz performers. In Memphis, I qualified but missed the cut. The next week I missed qualifying for the Western Open, but luckily we had a place to stay and practice in Milwaukee with friends, Barry Burdick and his wife, Jan. Barry was one of the Milwaukee guys that I met in Las Vegas. I shot 66 in the Monday qualifier and finally made my first cut after six tries, winning the grand total of $434. It wasn't even enough to pay my expenses. Today making the cut in the smallest tournament makes more than 10 times that for last place.

PGA TOUR MONDAY QUALIFYING

The rest of the year was uneventful. I won only $2,300 for the year on the Tour, but made the last cut at Pensacola, which got me into the first event in 1982 at Tucson. There were only six spots available at Tucson and the West Coast was always a tough swing to make qualifiers. A lot of good players and not many qualifying spots.

When the 1982 Florida swing began, I was running out of money fast and I owed about $3,000 on my credit card. I needed a sponsor. A friend of mine once said the easiest guy to beat is a broke PGA Tour player. I resembled that comment.

Gary Sorenson had given me $3,000 to get started and my parents had given me $6,000 toward the end of 1981. All of that was gone. I was at home, in tears, sitting out on the deck with my mom wondering how I was going to continue. I didn't even have the money to drive to Greensboro and enter the Monday qualifying.

As fate would have it, Brad Bryant had just finished tied for third at The Players Championship and his sponsors had recouped all their money. They were looking to sponsor another guy. Cindy Christmas was a friend of mine from college who lived at Errol Estate in Apopka. Her dad overheard Bryant's sponsors talking in the golf shop and said, "I've got your guy. His name is Larry Rinker." I met with one of them, Sandy Letterman, a few days later and he and a business partner, Dr. Joe Uricchio, agreed to sponsor me.

In the beginning they agreed to give me $2,000 a month, which wasn't enough to cover my expenses, but it certainly helped. I got to keep 20 percent of what I made, and when they got their money back, we split the profits 50-50.

THE JOURNEYMAN

The best player on the mini-tours in Florida was a guy named Larry Mowry. He would go on to have a great Senior Tour career and win five times, including the 1989 PGA Seniors' Championship. In 1982 he started helping me with my game and gave me a book called "Illusions" by Richard Bach, to help me envision my potential. Larry and I went out and played one day and after I got it 7 under he said, "Keep it going, shot for shot, don't let up." I shot my lowest score ever, 62, ten under.

The first tournament I played in after I got sponsored was in Mississippi. I qualified but missed the cut. In the second tournament back on Tour in Tallahassee I qualified, shot 62 in the first round and was leading by four. I didn't finish in the top 25, but it was my first time leading a PGA Tour event.

The U.S. Open in 1982 was at Pebble Beach and I started fantasizing about winning it by saying "I'm going to win the U.S. Open." With two levels of qualifying for the Open – local and sectional – I told myself, "I can't win the Open unless I am in the Open." When I went out jogging, I kept repeating, "I'm winning the Open." I got through both stages of qualifying. I also qualified for the Tour stop in Memphis, but missed the cut. Silver lining: I got to go to Pebble early.

I flew to Santa Barbara, Calif., and visited my friend Mitch Kemper, who had moved back to the Golden State. That night I walked outside and started swinging in the front yard. I thought if I stayed behind the ball, I couldn't hit it to the right and if I didn't turn it over, I couldn't hit it left. I was excited and I couldn't wait to try my new formula at Pebble Beach.

PGA TOUR MONDAY QUALIFYING

Rinker's 62 New Tally Record

By ELGIN WHITE
Tribune correspondent

TALLAHASSEE — Second-year pro Larry Rinker, former University of Florida golfer from Orlando, fired a course-record 10-under par 62 Thursday in the first round of the 14th annual Tallahassee Open to take a four-stroke lead over Hal Sutton, DeWitt Weaver and Tommy Armour, all with 66.

Rinker's record round included eight birdies and an eagle on the par-five 17th hole on Killearn Country Club's 7,027 yard course. The previous record of 63 was set by Joe Inman in 1974 and matched by Arnold Palmer in 1976.

Rinker collected only $2,729 in his first year on the tour in 1981, and has pocketed just a little over $600 so far this year.

His record round took a lot of glamour away from Sutton, who canned eight birdies himself in his round of 66, but he bogied the tough par-three 14th and the final hole when his tee shot found a divot hole.

"This is certainly the best round of golf I have ever played," Rinker said afterward. "I only missed one green, the 11th, but I got it up and down all right. These greens are putting beautifully, you can be aggressive on most of them...only a couple you have to be careful on."

Holding a two-stroke edge over the fast closing Sutton going into the 17th, Rinker put a 3-wood shot seven feet from the pin and calmly sank it for his eagle that set up his record score. He had a chance to get one more on the 18th, but a 20-foot birdie putt just missed right.

Rinker qualified for the tournament on Monday by shooting a 68, and said, "that's when I started playing good. I got the feeling. Today was the best I have hit it in a long time."

Ed Sneed, the 1977 Tallahassee Open champion, was an early round leader with a 67 and is considered a prime threat to be the only two-time winner here. Other former champions were not close. Allen Miller had a 74, Chi Chi Rodriguez also had a 74, Rik Massengale 71, Gary Koch 76, Mark Pfeil 69 and Barry Jaeckel a 71.

1982 1st round Tallahassee Open

On Sunday in a practice round, I had Pebble Beach pretty much all to myself. It felt like a scene out of one of my favorite books, "Golf in the Kingdom." I hit the ball well and noticed with my new move that the ball was flying straight with a little fade. I felt ready. I had told myself for the last two months that I was going to win the Open. There was something about Pebble that I felt comfortable with. Maybe it was the way the course set up, maybe it was the beauty of the ocean and all the creatures living there, or maybe it was because I could visualize every shot I wanted to hit on that golf course.

THE JOURNEYMAN

The first round I got a great tee time before 8 a.m. I played pretty well the first day and shot 74, making a great bogey on No. 16. The Open is a test of all your abilities, and you will be tested. The leader after the first day was Bruce Devlin with a 71.

My tee time on Friday was at 11:45 and I did something that morning that I had never done in my career. I made my travel plans to leave on Monday, because I was going to win the Open. Normally I would wait to see how I played and then make my travel arrangements. If I missed the cut, it would cost me to change my flight, and I would have to get to New York by Sunday to play a practice round for the next Monday qualifier at Westchester. But I was going to win the Open!

On the first hole I had an eight-foot putt for par, and I said, "I'm not missing this putt." Sure enough, I made it. Then I eagled No. 2, birdied 3 and 4, bogeyed 5 and birdied 6 and 7. I was 5 under after seven holes! I made a few bogeys in the tough stretch from 8 through 12, but birdied 16-17-18 coming in for a 67, the low round of that Open (which was later tied by Lanny Wadkins on Sunday). I was now in second place and going to play in the final group on Saturday with the leader, Bruce Devlin, who was in at 141 after a 70.

I floated into the media tent on Cloud 9. After a few questions about "how does it feel" to be playing in the last group tomorrow, I told the world media that "the U.S. Open is an illusion. It's just another tournament. I've played against these guys every week on the PGA Tour. Just because all you guys come here and cover it, makes it a big deal. That's the way I have to think of this tournament to deal with it. I do realize that it's the best tournament that there is."

PGA TOUR MONDAY QUALIFYING

They never heard the last two sentences. Headlines the next day said, "Rinker calls U.S. Open an illusion. Maybe he's an illusion."

1982 was one of the first times the U.S. Open television coverage was for all 18 holes on the weekend. When they finally announced my name on the first tee, Dave Marr commented, "That's a long time for Larry to be waiting. He called the Open an illusion, but I think that's kind of like whistling through the graveyard." I was so pumped up I hit 3-wood/sand wedge to the first hole and made par. I birdied No. 2 with a two-putt and after Devlin bogeyed No. 4, I was tied for the lead at 4 under. That was the last time I was tied. I bogeyed 5 and double-bogeyed 9 to shoot 75 and sit at even par for the tournament. Tom Watson was leading at 4 under and Jack Nicklaus was only a couple of shots back.

On Sunday I was playing well until I hit it out of bounds on No. 11 and made double bogey. I also double-bogeyed No. 14 after burying it in the front bunker. After I teed off on No. 15, Larry Guest of the Orlando Sentinel came up to me and said, "Hey Larry, if you play the last four holes 2 under you can qualify for the Masters!" I told Larry I had just double-bogeyed 14 and he said, "OK, play them 3 under."

I birdied 15 and 16 and on the par-three 17th I hit it to four feet with a 4-wood baffler! I missed the putt, however. On 18 I had a four-footer for par and said, "I will not be denied." I made it and went back to where I was staying. I ended up T-15, good enough to qualify for the 1983 Masters and U.S. Open. The Masters was top 16, and the U.S. Open was top 15. Tom Watson won his first and only U.S. Open, beating Nicklaus by two shots with an incredible chip-in on No. 17!

THE JOURNEYMAN

During my career on the PGA Tour, I liked to walk through the self-help section of bookstores and read a lot of books. I also ended up working with Dr. Bob Rotella and Dick Coop, who both worked with a lot of Tour players. Committing to winning the U.S. Open for months paid off with my first top-25. I won $4,500.

The next stop was the Westchester Classic in New York. I had just teed off on No. 2 in my practice round when I saw Payne Stewart playing No. 18. He ran over, scissor-kicked over the gallery ropes and said, "Way to go!" I couldn't believe how excited he was. He said, "Well, I'm gonna have to win a tournament. I can't let you play those practice rounds at the Masters alone." Payne won the Quad Cities Classic that summer and it was the only tournament that his dad got to see him win.

At the Sammy Davis Jr. Greater Hartford Open, I met two gentlemen, Kurt Godiksen and Bob Olesak, on the range and asked them where I could get some good seafood. They said that they knew a place and offered to take me. We went and it became an annual meal and get-together during the tournament. Kurt is a graphic art designer and started a fan club, The Connecticut Contingent of "Rinker's Drinkers," and the Hub of Rinkermania, which is an intense desire for Rinker-style golf. T-shirts were made and we had a lot of fun with it and ate at a lot of great restaurants. The south end of Hartford was known for its fine Italian restaurants, and there were a lot of them on Franklin Avenue.

A month later was the Bank of Boston Classic in Sutton, Massachusetts. Ted Mingolla, the owner of Pleasant Valley, always liked to invite top local amateurs before and after they turned pro like

PGA TOUR MONDAY QUALIFYING

Billy Andrade and Brad Faxon. There was an "old school" clambake for the players and families with live music. It was always fun to eat steamers, crack open lobster, and sit in with the band.

Playing the amateur circuit in the summers, we were used to inquiring about private housing. They would open up their homes to total strangers. I did this at the Northeast Amateur, the Western Amateur, and then at the Western Open where I stayed with Dr. Richard Polisner. At Pleasant Valley, I met Mike and Betty Feen, who I stayed with 18 years in a row. Mike did club repair in their basement and they were the best. Unfortunately, the tournament would end in 1998 and there were tears from all of us. We had become family. CVS, the sponsor in the final years, would start the CVS Health Charity Classic in Providence, R.I., hosted by Brad Faxon and Billy Andrade in 1999.

I played well the rest of the summer and in the last tournament at Walt Disney World I had a chance with nine holes to play to make the top 125. This was the all-exempt Tour that had been proposed by Gary McCord. No more Monday qualifying in 1983. Make the top 125 on the money list and you are in all the tournaments except the majors and invitationals. Everyone now could play in Monday pro-ams for extra money and life was a lot easier for most of the guys.

The only guys who lost out were those who didn't finish in the top 125 or make Q-School. No more Monday qualifying for PGA Tour members on the tournament courses. Only truly open qualifiers for four spots that anyone with a 2-handicap or less could play in at an off-site course.

THE JOURNEYMAN

After I birdied No. 10 on Sunday at Disney, I needed to play the last eight holes 1 under to make the top 125. I played them 2 over and finished 133rd on the money list. Tour school would be in Ponte Vedra Beach, Fla., at the TPC Stadium course and Sawgrass Country Club in November. It took $28,787 to make the top 125 in 1982. I ended up making that Q-School and finishing 24th. Fifty guys got their cards. Donnie Hammond won it by 14 shots and could have shot 103 the last round and made it! I was back on Tour.

In 1983, Mickey Neal, who had been the golf coach at Palm Beach Gardens High School, was now the MacGregor rep on Tour and he offered me an opportunity to join the MacGregor staff. In those days a lot of the companies just had bonus pools based on performance for the year.

I would be the 24th player eligible from the Q-School all year. The all-exempt Tour or priority Tour was a reality now. I was in the Masters and U.S. Open and eligible to play in Monday pro-ams, both at the tournament, and off-site around the country. This plus the manufacturers' bonus pools is how we survived until we started finishing higher on the money list.

Everyone was so excited to be at Augusta. I remember driving down Washington Road. It could have been any street in America. McDonalds, Pizza Hut, Burger King – all the chains were represented. Then you turned and there was a little guard house. I gave my name to the attendant and he said, "Welcome to Augusta National." Payne would say later in his life, just before he passed away in a mysterious plane crash, that "Sometimes you get to live out your dreams." My dream was that the first time I went to the Masters I would be playing in the tournament. Then I drove down Magnolia Lane and parked my car.

1983 Masters practice round: Larry with Payne Stewart and Scott Hoch on the first tee

Payne and I played that practice round with Scott Hoch. It was the first year that the players could bring their own caddies. My friend Mitch Kemper was caddying for Payne and Sandy McIntyre was my regular caddie. I didn't play well in the tournament, but it really didn't matter. I was in heaven on earth. The par-three tournament on Wednesday: All the former champions were there – Gary, Jack and Arnie and everybody else.

At the Byron Nelson, which was being played for the first time at the Robert Trent Jones Jr.-designed Las Colinas, I got paired with Jack on Saturday. I asked some friends if they had any advice and they said if you get a chance to putt out, do. Once Nicklaus finished a hole, the whole gallery would run to the next tee. I would shoot 79 that day and finish T-72.

THE JOURNEYMAN

I received a "Champion's Choice" exemption to the Colonial National Invitation in Fort Worth, Texas. The former champions get to pick two players who had never competed in the event before. Brandel Chamblee, who was playing in his first PGA Tour event, and Mark Brooks also received exemptions that year playing as amateurs. On Wednesday night Colonial had a former Champions dinner and we got invited. The three of us noticed that sitting up on the dais was none other than Ben Hogan. I had to go up and say hello. When I shook his large hand and said, "Hello, Mr. Hogan, I'm Larry Rinker," he said, "I've heard of you." Couldn't believe Hogan said that.

I finished 128th on the money list and it was back to Q-School. The Q-School in 1983 was again in Ponte Vedra Beach, but this time all six rounds would be played at the TPC Stadium Course. I opened with 79-76 and was in deep trouble. Going into the last round I needed to shoot 72. I just gave it to God and relaxed until I got to 16, 17 and 18. Then I couldn't breathe. I managed to par 16 and 17 and bogeyed 18 for 71 to make it with one shot to spare. My brother Lee finished a shot behind me and got his card on his first try.

Chapter 4

Best Years 1984-1985

BEST YEARS 1984-1985

1984 would be my breakout year, but in the beginning, I couldn't close out tournaments. At Pebble Beach I was paired with Jack Nicklaus and shot 83 on Sunday. At the Honda I was paired with Jack again on Sunday. When we walked off the first tee, Jack came up and put his arm around me and said, "You're not going to have that bad front nine again, are you?" I shot 42-37 for 79. I was OK with the galleries, the lights, the cameras, but pair me with my childhood idol and I really struggled. In Orlando the next week at the Bay Hill Classic I shot 81 on Sunday. In all these tournaments I was in the top 25 going into Sunday and at Bay Hill I was in the top 10!

1984 Honda Classic: Larry with Jack Nicklaus and Roger Maltbie in the final round at TPC Eagle Trace

THE JOURNEYMAN

The next tournament was in New Orleans. My brother Lee was having trouble getting into tournaments. In 1984 the Tour decided that the Q-School graduates would be reshuffled four times during the season, and Lee was at the bottom of the barrel. Lee had only two starts and New Orleans was his third tournament. Lee's teammate and college roommate at Alabama was Tommy Brennan from the famous Brennan family of New Orleans. They owned Commander's Palace as well as Brennan's in Houston, and Tommy's sister, Cindy, and brother, Ralph, had recently opened Mr. B's. I had stayed with Tommy's parents, John and Claire, in 1983, and now Lee and I were both staying with them for the tournament.

Going into the final round in New Orleans, I was tied for third and in the next-to-last group. On the first hole I hit my drive in the tree roots that were everywhere at Lakewood CC. I thought, here we go again on Sunday. But after making bogey I birdied the next four holes, shot 68, and finished second to Bob Eastwood. $43,200! I now had enough to pretty much guarantee I would finish in the top 125 for the year.

So as I watched the next week's Masters, I was feeling pretty good. The next event, the Sea Pines Heritage, is an invitational and I wasn't expecting to get in the field. My caddie called and said, "You're in!" I said, "I think I'll just take this week off," but he persuaded me to change my mind when he said, "You will love this place," referring to Hilton Head and Harbour Town Golf Links. So I flew up on Tuesday and played a practice round.

Was I ever glad I decided to play. I shot 67-70-68, which put me in the final group with Dr. Gil Morgan and Nick Faldo. My first final

BEST YEARS 1984-1985

group on Sunday, it was Easter, and I was nervous. I didn't play well and got bogeyed to death. Shot 77 and finished T-15. Nick Faldo won his first event on the PGA Tour.

I played well the rest of 1984, and in the next-to-last tournament, the Walt Disney World Golf Classic, I had another chance to win. On my bag was Greg Rita, who would win two U.S. Opens with Curtis Strange in 1988-89. I opened up with a solid 69 in the first round at the Magnolia course. After 15 holes on the Palm course I was 2 over for the day and 1 under for the tournament. I birdied the last three holes on the front nine to shoot 71. On Saturday I shot 64 at Lake Buena Vista, where I was hanging out and practicing in off weeks. Jon Brendle was the head golf professional there, before he went on to become a rules official on the PGA Tour.

Larry's winner's check from the 1984 Gator Pro-Am

Sunday, I shot 29 on the front nine and birdied No. 10 to go 8 under for the day and -20 for the tournament. That's 19 under for the last 31 holes. I ended up playing the last eight holes 3 over to shoot 67 and tie for sixth. Larry Nelson would win with -22. I had four top-10s and finished 60th on the money list, the old standard before the all-exempt Tour. I made $116,494 and I won the Gator Pro-Am in Gainesville before Christmas. But perhaps most significantly, I would not have to go to Q-School.

1985: Best year

For the first time in my career I was able to pretty much pick and choose tournaments. I was also going to be in the Wednesday pro-ams in more than half of the tournaments. Jack Nicklaus had given the MacGregor staff an ultimatum: If we wanted to be on staff, we had to play the Jack Nicklaus golf ball. Only Jack, myself and Chi Chi Rodriguez played the ball that year and he gave the rest of the staff one more year to make up their minds.

I flew into L.A. and rented a car for the first three weeks. The drive to Palm Springs for the Bob Hope tournament is about two hours; when you see the giant wind turbines you know you're getting close. I had never played in the Hope and I was staying with my older brother, Laine Jr., who had just moved there. His wife, Kellii, had just finished playing the LPGA Tour for four years and they were kind of starting over. Laine Jr. was returning to the mortgage business after traveling with Kellii on tour. I made the cut, finished T-53 and headed for Phoenix.

BEST YEARS 1984-1985

1982 Western Open: Larry with John O'Donnell as his caddie

I made another cut in Phoenix. On to L.A. On Wednesday, I played Bel-Air Country Club with John O'Donnell, who was on the golf team at UCLA. John, who today has his own clothing company, Johnnie O's, had caddied for me at the Western Open in 1982 when we used to use the Evans Scholars as caddies. John's brother is the actor Chris O'Donnell. At L.A. on Sunday, I was 2 over through six holes for the day, but I shot 69 (with a bogey on 18) and finished tied for seventh.

At Pebble Beach, my partner was my brother's roommate from college, Tommy Brennan from New Orleans. Having a scratch golfer for a partner in this event was an advantage, because we played the same tees, and he could hit first on the par-threes. The first round was at Cypress Point and we started on the 10th tee. The 15th hole was playing straight down wind and Tommy hit a 9-iron over the green. After witnessing that, I hit a pitching wedge, which was the right club for the 154-yard hole. We couldn't believe it was the right club!

1985 Bing Crosby National Pro-Am: From L to R, Jodie Mudd, Jodie's partner, Larry, Tommy Brennan

After eight holes I was 4 over par for the round and the wind was really starting to blow. Somehow, I got it all the way back to even par with just the ninth hole to play. Nine was playing straight down gale and I hit a 3-wood in the green-side bunker on the par-four. I was not able to get the ball on the green and ended up making bogey and shooting 1 over. Even-par 72 was the low round and the horror stories were starting to come in. My friend Nathaniel Crosby had it under par heading into 14 and ended up shooting 78. Hal Sutton shot 87.

BEST YEARS 1984-1985

The next day I shot 72 at Spyglass and got ready for Pebble Beach. On Saturday I shot 69 and was in about 30th place heading into the final round. My pairing was Greg Norman, Bernhard Langer and Kikio Arai from Japan. I hit it into the ocean at 4 and 10 and was just in the middle of the pack heading into 14. I birdied 14 and on 16 CBS showed me hitting my second shot just over the green. When they showed me again on the 17th tee, I was 1 more under. On 17, CBS showed me hitting my tee shot into the right-hand bunker. They next showed me hitting my third shot into 18 and once again I was 1 more under.

On 18 my third shot ended up about 15 feet right of the hole. Greg Norman had reached the par-five in two and just missed his eagle putt. I told my caddie if we make this one, we can "pull up a chair." I poured it right into the middle of the cup and ended up birdieing four out of the last five holes at Pebble Beach! Kikio Arai had tied me and I beat Norman and Langer.

Mark O'Meara had a one-stroke lead playing 18. Mark and Curtis Strange both hit it about 12 feet at 18. Curtis had a putt to tie Mark and missed it. Mark then two-putted for a one-stroke victory over Curtis, Arai and me. After four events I had won more than $50,000 and that was enough to make the top 125 for the year. Some start as I drove to San Francisco to fly to Hawaii.

Landing in Hawaii on Monday, I was on Cloud 9. My friend Will Hurley, the piano player from Ponte Vedra, had moved there recently, and followed me in my practice round. On the sixth hole, I noticed that Arnold Palmer was playing by himself in front of me. Mr. Palmer waved me up to join him. When we finished the ninth hole, I asked Mr. Palmer if he was going to play the back nine. He said, "I am if you are." That night, Arnold, his wife, Winnie, and his chief architect, Ed Seay, came out to the restaurant to listen to me sit in with Will and his band! Arnold Palmer had a way to make everyone around him feel great. His parting words to me that night were "Go win!"

1985 in Hawaii: L to R, Will Hurley, John Kirkland, Larry

TPC Stadium course

Will Hurley had moved back to Florida and was playing music most nights, including a gig in a tent at the course during The Players. I knew the course well, having survived Q-Schools in 1982 and 1983. I had played in The Players in 1984, not to mention the other times I had gone up to practice during the day and sit in and play music with Will at night.

BEST YEARS 1984-1985

After rounds of 68-72, I found myself in the second-to-last group with the eventual winner, Calvin Peete. I had heard that Calvin couldn't putt, but after missing the third green, he had a 10-footer for par. No problem, swish. Calvin at one point in the 1980s had won more events that decade than any other player. Yes, he could putt, and he led the driving accuracy stat for 10 straight years, 1981-1990, despite having a permanently bent left arm, the result of a childhood accident.

In those days they didn't overseed the fairways at TPC, and they were firm and fast. I shot 71 in the third round and again was in the penultimate group with Gary Hallberg on Sunday. Gary and I were battling it out that day and when we got to 16, we realized Calvin Peete and D.A. Weibring had made some birdies, and we were now playing for third. I parred the last two holes and ended up finishing third alone for my biggest check on Tour, $61,200. I was currently eighth on the 1985 money list.

Heading into the PGA Championship at Cherry Hills in Denver, I was 19th in Ryder Cup points. I didn't play well and missed the cut. After a few weeks off, I went back on Tour and made the cut in the first two events. The next event was the Greater Milwaukee Open. After rounds of 68-70-68 I was once again in the penultimate group. Jack Nicklaus and the eventual winner, Jim Thorpe, were in the final pairing. With a birdie and holing my second shot for eagle on the fourth hole, I was tied for the lead with Jim Thorpe heading into the back nine.

On 17, I buried my tee shot in the left-hand bunker by the green and ended up making double. That cost me tying Nicklaus for second and I ended up tied for third with four other players.

I finished the year out with four made cuts and three top-16s to end up 31st on the money list. Seve Ballesteros had played in only nine events and by our bylaws he was required to play in 15. When our commissioner, Deane Beman, asked him to play in more events, Seve declined. So Beman removed him from the money list and now I was officially 30th and waiting to hear from the Masters and USGA to see if I would be in their tournaments in 1986.

There were two team events in December: the J. C. Penney Classic, which was a mixed team event I played with my sister Laurie, and the Chrysler Team Championship, where I partnered with Jay Haas. After having come somewhat close to winning, I was bound and determined to win the J.C. Penney Classic. Before Thanksgiving I started committing to win that event.

Laurie had qualified for the LPGA Tour in July of 1982 and was that tour's youngest player at 19. In 1984 she won her first tournament, the Boston Five, and finished 12th on the LPGA money list. In 1985 she had another solid year, finishing in the top 30 on the money list. She would win her second LPGA Tour event later in 1986 at the Corning Classic and have a stretch where she finished in the top 16 on the money list in 1984, 1986 and 1987. She was bound and determined to win the J.C. Penney Classic as well.

The J.C. Penney Classic had a future Hall of Famers field. Curtis Strange and Nancy Lopez were both players of the year on their respective tours and teamed together. The field also included Greg Norman and Sally Little, Tom Kite and Beth Daniel, Tom Purtzer and Julie Inkster, Craig Stadler and Lori Garbacz, Andy Bean and Amy Benz, and many others. My brother Lee was caddying for Laurie and he told me at the beginning of the week to "leave her alone. I got her." We opened with a 66 in the first round, and before we played the second round on Friday, I got word that Augusta National was going to invite me to play in the 1986 Masters, since I was "officially" in the top 30 on the money list for 1985. Yeah!!!

We shot 68 on Friday and 67 on Saturday and found ourselves in the final group on Sunday with Mark McCumber and Chris Johnson, who was walking the fairways backward because of an injury. We stayed in the lead or tied for most of the front nine until we birdied No. 9 to go one ahead and take the lead to the back nine. We knew we needed more birdies to win but patience was going to be key.

After a string of pars, we birdied the difficult par-three 13th hole and were still in the lead. Nancy Lopez and Curtis Strange were making a move and it seemed like every time they made a birdie, we answered. We birdied 13 and the par-five 16th, which kept us two strokes ahead of Lopez and Strange, who were now on 18. Curtis flew his third shot into the hole on the par-five 18th, but it bounced out and came to a stop about 15 feet away. If it had stayed in for eagle, they would have tied us. Instead, they two-putted for par and we still had them by two strokes.

(left) 1985: Front page of Golfweek, (right) 1986: Front page of Golfweek

Laurie and I both hit good drives on 17 and both hit nice approaches into the green. Laurie was closest so it was my turn to putt. I buried the putt for birdie, and we had a two-shot lead with one hole to play! The 18th was a three-shot par-five and after two shots one of us had to hit the third shot into the green. Laurie played the third shot with a sand wedge into the green and hit it about 15 feet short of the flagstick. Two putts later we had shot a 66 to finish -21, and we had won the J.C. Penney Classic by two shots over Craig Stadler and Lori Garbacz!!! A win, finally!!!

After Laurie's and my J.C. Penney win, our father would be named "Golf Father of the Year" by Golfweek magazine. The win was "unofficial," but I officially became a member of the PGA Tour for life with the win. It didn't mean I was going to get in any more tournaments, just that I had membership and membership has its privileges. Now with the all-exempt Tour there were basically three categories of membership for life: tournament winners, mixed team tournament winners, and players who had made 150 career cuts.

Later in the early '90s the PGA Tour created a life membership for players who had won 20 or more tournaments. That meant they were in any regular PGA Tour event for as long as they wanted to play. 1985, what a year! I also led the Tour with the most eagles, 14. Guess who finished second? Corey Pavin. Now on to 1986, where I was back in the Masters and the U.S. Open at Shinnecock.

Chapter 5

Stephen Stills Tour – All Access

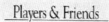

Players & Friends

Rinker & Stills Make Sweet Music

By George Whittier
PHOTOGRAPHY BY STAN BADZ / PGA TOUR

One plays the guitar and dabbles in golf, the other plays golf and dabbles in the guitar. Their friendship is a natural.

PGA TOUR veteran Larry Rinker and music superstar Stephen Stills, most notably of the rock group Crosby, Stills, Nash and Young, go together like the strings of a guitar.

Actually, Rinker might have been a professional guitarist himself. The Beatles inspired him at age 8 to start playing and during his high school days in Stuart, FL, he was a member of a group that once performed in front of 2,000 people.

"That was pretty much the highlight of my musical career," Rinker said.

Stills is an avid golfer, if not a proficient one. He confesses that he hasn't had any highlights yet on the golf course, certainly nothing to remotely compare to his reputation as a musician. In spite of his long string of hits in the '70s, though, he never did develop an ego.

"He's just an ordinary guy," Rinker said of his occasional playing partner on the golf course and the bandstand. "He's like me, he's got Florida roots. He lived in Lake Wales quite a long time. His nickname is 'Gator'. There's almost a mythology about Crosby, Stills, Nash and Young, but Stephen is just a person."

The two met in 1986 in Orlando, where Rinker now lives. Stills was at the Grand Cypress Resort, playing a round of golf. Paul Celano, then the Grand Cypress Resort director of golf, tipped Rinker off that the famed guitarist was at the course.

"So I went there and was playing the course, going down No. 2, while he was playing No. 6," Rinker said of the adjoining holes. "We ran into each other, started talking and ended up having dinner together.

"He came over to my house that night and played a few songs. I had always been a big fan of his but I became a

STEPHEN STILLS TOUR – ALL ACCESS

Jack Nicklaus' ultimatum was for real now about playing the MacGregor ball, and the only people left on the MacGregor staff were Jack, myself and Chi Chi Rodriguez.

In early January I got a call from a friend, Dennis Cone, who said that Stephen Stills was going to be out playing golf at the Grand Cypress resort that day. Grand Cypress had offered me, Payne Stewart and Greg Norman complimentary memberships. I met Stephen on the fifth tee of the East course, and I played the rest of the nine with him. After we finished, I gave Stephen a ride back to his hotel in Winter Park. We went out to eat and ended up at my house. Here I was sitting on my couch and Stephen Stills was playing music. I had a PA set up in the living room, so it was perfect. He taught me the song, "Make Love to You." Stephen ended up staying two more weeks in Orlando at Grand Cypress and a friendship was kindled. We played golf and music and had a lot of fun.

I started off 1986 missed cut, missed cut, missed cut, T-6 at San Diego, missed cut and T-33 at L.A., where Stephen Stills came out to Riviera and walked the fairways with me in the practice round. My friend Mitch Kemper was now working in L.A. for E.F. Hutton; they had a party for the pros who were clients, which included Steve Pate and Payne Stewart.

We decided to invite Stephen and the next thing we knew he was playing the piano for all of us. We ended up at Mitch's apartment and sang a bunch of Stephen's songs with him including "Love the

THE JOURNEYMAN

One You're With." Mitch and I got invited over to Stephen's house for dinner on Friday night where we met his son Christopher, who was quite the musician at age 11. We got to jam with him and hang out with Stephen. Stephen would end up hosting this event at his house for quite a few years. Lots of fun memories. The West Coast swing was over, and I had cemented my friendship with Stephen Stills.

1999 at Stephen Stills' house: L to R, Mitch Kemper, Stephen Stills, Harvey Mason, Larry, Geoff Couch

In the first round of the Masters, I hit my second shot on No. 1 just over the green. The hole was located in the back-left portion of the green and I got my chip shot barely on about 12 feet away. As I stood over the putt for par my ball moved. I called for a rules official and it was deemed that I had caused the ball to move and incurred a one-stroke penalty. Nobody saw it but me. I made the putt for bogey, birdied No. 2 and shot my best round at the Masters, 73.

STEPHEN STILLS TOUR – ALL ACCESS

The next day I missed some four-footers early and shot 81. Augusta National has the hardest set of greens that I have ever played. I have never played anywhere that I felt so uncomfortable. It ended up being a historic weekend where Jack Nicklaus rallied on Sunday and won his sixth green jacket at the age of 46. Yeah, that Masters.

1986 Masters, Par 3 Contest: Caddie Russ Craver

I made three out of the next four cuts and decided to take a week off after the Memorial to get ready for a five-week stretch that included the U.S. Open at Shinnecock. My life changed that week I took off. I met my soon-to-be wife, Janet Jackson, from Fort Lauderdale, Florida. We met at Dinky Dock on the Winter Park chain of lakes next to Rollins College. I had an attorney friend, Rick Troutman, who had a boat and we used to go skiing. Jan was a competitive skier who knew Rick and they were getting together to put some buoys in the ski course on Lake Virginia.

THE JOURNEYMAN

Jan owned a condo near my house in Winter Park, so everything was close by. I told her I was going out on the road for five weeks and hoped to see her when I got home. These were the days of no cell phones or email. Just call the home line.

I made the cut at Westchester and finished T-41. Now it was time to drive out to Long Island for the U.S. Open. Shinnecock Hills Golf Club in Southampton has a rich history: Opened in 1891, it became one of the five founding members of the United States Golf Association, and in 1896 it hosted the second U.S. Open. Remarkably, it hadn't hosted another Open until this one.

I was renting a house again with my mom and dad for the week. On Wednesday, the wind was fierce during the practice round, and it only increased for Thursday's first round, with gusts topping 40 mph. Bob Tway was the only player able to match par in that first round with a 70. I shot 77, which was middle of the field. Greg Norman managed to shoot 68 in the second round and held a one-stroke lead at 1 under. I shot 71 and made the cut. I would finish with a 70-71 on the weekend to finish T-24 at +9.

On the weekend, Greg Norman was the story. A blond, charismatic, long-hitting Australian who was on his way to becoming the No. 1-ranked player in the world, Norman was viewed by many as the heir to Jack Nicklaus. At Shinnecock, a third-round 71 sent Norman into the final 18 holes with a one-shot lead over Hal Sutton and Lee Trevino. It was Norman's second consecutive 54-hole lead in a major, as he had held a one-shot lead going into Sunday at the Masters. Norman would go on to lead after 54 holes at the British Open and PGA Championship, which led to the coining of the term "Saturday Slam."

STEPHEN STILLS TOUR – ALL ACCESS

Norman had three reasons to be hungry at Shinnecock: One, he was seeking his first major title. Two, he had come agonizingly close to winning a U.S. Open once before. In 1984 at Winged Foot, another historic New York golf club, Norman had holed a 45-foot par-saving putt on the 72nd hole that wound up getting him into a playoff with Fuzzy Zoeller, only to fall in the playoff, 67 to 75. And three, Norman had just come close to tasting victory at Augusta.

During the final round at Shinnecock, Norman was one of 10 players who either led or were tied for the lead. But he shot a disappointing 75 that left him six strokes behind the winner, 43-year-old Raymond Floyd, who closed with a 66. As he had done at the Masters, Norman again lost to the oldest player ever to win that particular event. He would finally break through at the British Open the following month, but that's getting ahead of ourselves.

After this five-week stretch, I got to go out on the road with Stephen Stills for four days, which was a bucket-list item. Traveling in Stephen's bus, going to sound checks with an all-access pass, I was part of the band. We hung out and stayed up most of the night playing music ("Daylight Again"). I got to watch the concerts standing next to Rance Caldwell at the stage monitor's board on Stephen's side, stage right. Stills was on a solo tour because David Crosby was serving time for a gun and drug possession conviction.

Meeting Stephen Stills lit a fire and I started playing out around Winter Park with a sax player named Walt at a place called Tim Webber's. The Pensacola Open was played the week before Disney and I had a gig set up for Monday night of Disney hoping some of the players would come down. After two rounds of the Pensacola

Open, I was T-17 with rounds of 69-67. We teed off on Saturday, played a few holes, and it started raining to the point where play was called for the day. The next day we never teed off and rain was in the forecast for the next two days.

1986 Donnie Hammond Pro-am with Stephen Stills and Walt

When Sunday's round was canceled and they were now going to finish on Monday, I went into the rules officials' trailer and asked what would happen if I withdrew? They said I would get a last-place check unless there were no more rounds completed, in which case I would still finish T-17. Since the purse was only $250,000, I gambled, flew home on Sunday, and played in the Oldsmobile Scramble Pro-am on Monday morning at the Disney Magnolia course.

They never played any more holes in Pensacola! Yes, this is the Ernie Gonzalez year, where he was awarded an official win for only two rounds. That regulation was later changed to require the completion of three rounds for an official win. When I saw Payne at the gig on Monday night, he said you're a pretty lucky guy. I had set up for Will Hurley to come down and we had a blast jamming with Payne on his harmonica.

As fate would have it, I played with Jack Nicklaus and Jack II in the Chrysler Team Championship the last round of the year. MacGregor was going through some changes with their golf ball and now a new company was making it. But there were problems, both with the distribution and the manufacturing quality of the balls.

If you were playing Titleist golf balls, the reps would put your balls in your locker every week. With MacGregor, I would have to go find them. At the Masters, I didn't get my MacGregor balls until Wednesday morning. It wasn't like they were being delivered from some far-away site – the factory was in Albany, Georgia! On another occasion I received balls that had not passed the USGA ball test and thus were illegal. (They submitted new ones that later were approved.) At Pleasant Valley, I hit a 4-iron into the wind that went only 150 yards. Something was up, so I contacted the president of MacGregor and we came to a verbal agreement that I could play whatever ball I wanted until they got their problems sorted out.

At the Chrysler, Jack sees that I am not playing his ball and instead I'm using a Maxfli DDH. He is not happy. He says we need to talk after the round. The Nicklauses played well, finishing T-4. TV wanted to do an interview, but Jack wanted to talk to me first. I told him, "You don't know what goes on out here when you're not out." I told him about the Masters and about the 4-iron that went only 150 yards. He was unmoved. "I don't care if your driver is going 150 yards, you need to make a decision," he said. So I made that decision. I relinquished my MacGregor staff deal and played the Maxfli DDH the next year.

After I drove back to Winter Park from south Florida things were going well. Jan and I were dating, and I was glad to be home for the holidays. 1986 will be remembered as a great year because it was the year I met Stephen Stills and most importantly, the year I met my future wife.

In 1987 the Phoenix Open was moved from Phoenix Country Club downtown, to the new TPC design by Tom Weiskopf in the suburb of Scottsdale. At the country club they had a hospitality area, the "Birds Nest," short for Thunderbirds, who ran the tournament. It had live bands and could accommodate several hundred people. At TPC Scottsdale it could hold thousands, and they hired a band from Austin, Texas, "Duck Soup," led by Sam Irwin.

With such a great field, other tournament hosts would come to Phoenix to recruit, and when they saw the Birds Nest, they wanted to have a great party atmosphere and killer entertainment tent at their tournaments, too. "Duck Soup" became the unofficial band of the PGA Tour, playing at many other Tour stops. I got to sit in with them all over the place through the years. The Birds Nest today boasts four nights of live entertainment with national acts and has earned legendary status on the PGA Tour. It offers a show all its own and is totally unlike anything else associated with professional golf.

The 1987 Doral-Ryder Open was one of the first million-dollar purses. After a 66-71, I was in the final group on Saturday with Bernhard Langer. On a windy day I finished bogey, triple bogey to shoot 76 on Saturday and be in 12th place heading into the final round. If I had parred 18, I would have been in the last group. About 1 in the morning I woke up feeling violently ill. Food poisoning. Jan rushed me to the Baptist Hospital emergency room, where I stayed for four or five hours.

Early Sunday morning they released me from the hospital, but I had no energy. There was no way I could play, much less walk 18 holes. I called the Tour officials and withdrew from the tournament. I was so weak we didn't even drive home that day. Once we did get home the next day, I withdrew from the next tournament on the schedule, the Honda Classic.

Back in Winter Park, Jan took care of me, made me her "marry me" chicken noodle soup, and I said, this is the woman I want taking care of me for the rest of my life. I was in love, wanted to get married and needed to get a ring. My dad helped me find one and I proposed to Jan on Friday night of the Masters.

Being raised Southern Baptist I was looking for a place for us to get married and we started attending the First Baptist Church of Winter Park. We found out that if we were members, we could save $100 on the cost of the marriage ceremony, so we joined!

We were married in July and on our honeymoon at the Florida Open at Innisbrook, I worked with Peter Kostis, who I had worked with on and off going back to 1984. From my journal:

> Turn setting hands and wrists going back
> Swing down from the top and let arms separate from body. Keep body back. If body turns too soon on forward swing, I'll hit left to left hooks or push fades.

THE JOURNEYMAN

Boy, if I had only stayed with that, because that is all correct for the way my swing works.

After getting married I felt that I needed to step up my game as the leader of our household and read the entire Life Application Bible along with the study notes. I started going to Sunday school again and playing music at the First Baptist Church of Winter Park.

Chapter 6

Bob Rotella and Fender Music

BOB ROTELLA AND FENDER MUSIC

In 1988 Deane Beman asked me to put a band together to perform for the players and their families at the annual barbeque at The Players Championship. I always traveled with my guitar – I checked my clubs but I carried my guitar on the plane. I would sit in all over the place; what better way to pass the time than play guitar? Mark Lye played guitar, Payne Stewart played harmonica, and Peter Jacobsen could entertain anyone, so he was our lead singer. John Inman sang in a barbershop quartet, so he was one of our back-up singers.

1988: Jake Trout and the Flounders' first gig, Ponte Vedra Beach at The Players

On Wednesday night of the Bay Hill Classic, I invited Peter over to see what we could come up with. We came up with a blues song where Peter ad-libbed and made fun of the Tour. We did a parody of "Twist and Shout" where Peter named every Hispanic player on the planet. Mark Lye was friends with Eric Clapton, so they came up with "Slow Play," to the tune of Clapton's hit "Cocaine." We had three songs. Somewhere in the next seven days we became "Jake Trout and the Flounders."

I contacted my friend Will Hurley to get us a backup band. Peter did a great job and we ended up being quite the hit, so much so that we were invited to play at the FedEx St. Jude Classic Pro-am party in Memphis in August.

We took advantage of the time to come up with more songs. I remember having the guys over at the Buick Open. We were like Weird Al Yankovic doing golf parodies of some of our friends' songs. "Defenders of the Flag" by Bruce Hornsby became "Attackers of the Flag." "Sitting On the Dock of the Bay" became "Hitting On the Back of the Range," and so on.

We needed another backup band for this gig and Mark Lye put his good friend, Donald "Duck" Dunn, on the case. He came up with a local Memphis band, Human Radio. Duck was a member of Booker T. & the M.G.'s and a session player for Stax Records, where he played on thousands of songs. He also was the bass player for the Blues Brothers. One of my fondest memories is rehearsing for the gig with Duck at his house, just the two of us.

The band was now Peter, Payne, Mark and me. CBS came out and recorded the gig and Bob Drum interviewed us for his "Drummer's Beat" segment for that weekend's coverage. Now the Tour was asking us if we could play the awards party at the Tournament of Champions the following January at La Costa.

BOB ROTELLA AND FENDER MUSIC

1988, Memphis: Jake Trout and the Flounders' second gig. L to R, Fluff Cowan, Payne, Larry, Mark Lye, Donald "Duck" Dunn

A few weeks later at the Canadian Open I had my second-best stretch of golf on the Tour. After a 77 the first round, I shot back-to-back 65s. On Sunday after eight holes I was 4 under for the round. Let's see, that's 18 under par for 44 holes. I got around to the 13th tee and they blew the horn for a weather delay. I was in second place with three par-fives ahead of me. They ended up calling it for the day and we finished on Monday. Sunday was nice – high 70s and no wind. Monday it was in the 50s and blowing 20-30 mph. I parred 13, triple-bogeyed 14, shot 72 and finished T-7. Ken Green was the eventual winner.

In the summertime, a lot of the top players would take time off, which left their caddies available. I started having "Golf Ball" caddie for me at some of the tournaments. Golf Ball – real name Dolphus Hull, but nobody called him that – had caddied for Raymond Floyd and now he was on Calvin Peete's bag.

At the B.C. Open in 1988 I had a 9:28 tee time on Saturday. The minute hand ticked relentlessly toward the bottom of the hour, and still no Golf Ball. I checked the caddie tent for an emergency replacement, but no one was available.

Then my wife came to my rescue – four months pregnant with our first child. Lugging my 40-pound bag down the first fairway, she made it clear that I would have to keep up with her, not the other way around. "Come on," she said. "Let's get it going."

After I hit my tee shot on No. 6, here comes Golf Ball strolling nonchalantly into the fairway, devouring a local sandwich delicacy known as a spiedie, which is basically a shish kebob in a sub roll. He told me he had overslept. As he approached Jan to take the bag, she said, "I got this." I said, "Honey, Ball has the bag." Reluctantly she gave it up, but not before reminding us that she had gotten me to 1 under through five holes. Word got out about the situation and the local newspaper interviewed her about it after the round.

In retrospect, I shouldn't have been surprised by Golf Ball's late arrival. Two weeks previously in Milwaukee, the tournament director had told me that Golf Ball was in jail. He also told me not to worry, that the tournament would bail him out in time for him to caddie for me in Round 1. That was a bit of a stretch, as he didn't show up until I was in the ninth fairway. I was using a local caddie, and I told Golf Ball that he would have to pay the guy for working nine holes. "Is 20 dollar OK?" he asked. I just shook my head.

BOB ROTELLA AND FENDER MUSIC

My association with Golf Ball ended the week after the B.C. Open when he whiffed the first round (that's Tour-speak for "didn't show up") at the Southern Open. When he finally arrived on the third hole I told him, "That's strike three … and you're out."

Caddying is often said to have three commandments: Show up, keep up and shut up. If you can't obey the first one, the other two really don't matter.

Jan wasn't the only Tour wife who could shoulder a bag when necessary. That was nice, but what really gave me peace of mind was the amazing job she did taking care of our home and our kids. When I was on the road without her, I knew I could focus solely on my golf game and not have to worry about anything else. Still, it was great when she and the kids were able to join me on the road, which, once the children reached school age, was limited to the summer.

During this summer I had the best cut streak of my career, making 12 cuts in a row. I was just having trouble closing tournaments out. Many times I was playing the last five holes 2 or 3 over. At the end of that cut streak, I had a chance to win at the Southern Open. I was paired with Payne Stewart on Sunday and after 14 holes, I needed to play the last four holes in just 1 under to get into a playoff. I played them 3 over, shot 69 and finished T-14. It was time to go see Bob Rotella.

I flew into Charlottesville, Va., on Friday, stayed through the weekend and flew home on Sunday. Here are some of my notes from my time with Bob Rotella:

THE JOURNEYMAN

Want to get mindset and physical working together. Relax and Trust. Hard to visualize in pressure situations.

Need to learn to play without visualization. Mindset. Only care about scoring. Enjoy playing golf.

Behind the ball-totally and decisively make up my mind that the ball is going to the target. Don't have to visualize.

Commit to the decision and lock eyes and mind into the target. Mind can distract the eyes. Any distraction walk away. Accept you should be nervous.

Don't think about golf in between shots. Leave golf at the golf course. Don't think about golf until you go into the locker room. It's important to be refreshed.

Greatness takes total attention. If you let go you win. Instead of trying harder let go. During a round, tournament, and career, always be moving freer and looser, cockier, and more decisive. Have faith that looser and freer works.

Routine – From the last look at the target to setting the head to pulling the trigger, this time wants to get real constant. Very important to commit to doing this all the time.

Have to be good at forgiving and forgetting. After this you can accept and trust. Now you can let it go.

This is directly opposite of being hard on yourself and working on your faults. This is great for technical efficiency, but in doing this it destroys confidence and trust.

BOB ROTELLA AND FENDER MUSIC

> Must trust what you train. Don't care what anyone thinks. Don't care what other people are doing either. Free it up and let it go instead of getting careful.

I again made the top 125, finishing 95th on the money list, and Jan and I would have our first child, Devon, in November of 1988. It was one of the greatest days of my life seeing the birth of my son. We were so excited. My entire image of myself changed. Now I was a father, with all of the responsibilities that come with that life change.

1989 Bob Hope Classic L to R Laine Jr, Jan Rinker, Larry holding Devon, Glen Campbell, Kellii Rinker

In 1989 Jan, Devon, and I started the year off flying to Sacramento, Calif., and getting a van to use for the next five weeks. At the Team Championship in December I had played with a Chrysler dealer who said that we could use a vehicle for the West Coast swing. We drove down to La Costa to play the Jake Trout and the Flounders gig at the awards party at the Tournament of

THE JOURNEYMAN

Champions. Let's just say that we were starting to have different opinions as to how Jake Trout and the Flounders was going to operate, and it just wasn't feeling right. I had decided before I got to California that I was going to quit the band after that gig, even though it broke my heart.

I started off missing the cut in four of the first five tournaments through Doral. I was not feeling confident at all about my game. I started listening to a Christian radio station driving back and forth from the Honda Classic at TPC Eagle Trace to my mother-in-law's condo in Fort Lauderdale. I dedicated to God that I was going to tithe 10 percent of what I won that week to the radio station along with my regular tithe to my home church. I played in the penultimate group on Sunday and finished T-13 with a final-round 74. I was in the penultimate group on Sunday again the following week at Bay Hill, shot another 74 and finished T-8. I would go on to make nine cuts in a row! My, how things can turn around in golf.

At the Colonial in Fort Worth, Texas, I used to stay with Peter Snyder, who was a pretty good piano player. We had a lot of fun playing every year, and in 1989 I noticed he was playing quite a bit better. He was taking piano lessons. Well, there was no way I was going to let him get ahead of me, so when I got home, I contacted a jazz saxophonist named Eddie Marshall to help me find a guitar teacher. I had met Eddie the year before at Disney when we were trying to do a Jake Trout and the Flounders show. Peter and Payne couldn't make it, so Mark Lye and I did the gig for Nabisco.

Eddie Marshall introduced me to Steve Luciano, a guitar player who was a regular at Disney World and played in the "Kids of the

Kingdom" band. I told Steve I wanted to learn how to play single-note jazz and understand the theory behind the music. We started with "Misty" and it went from there. I used to play scales watching "SportsCenter" on ESPN.

1988 Disney World: L to R, Eddie Marshall, Larry, Christine Hurley, Goofy, Will Hurley, Mark Lye, Barry Smith

One of the great things about getting off to a decent start is that you could afford to take a couple of weeks off from the Tour and go over to the UK and try to qualify for the British Open. On May 30, I received a fax offering me a sponsor's exemption to the Scottish Open at Gleneagles. I flew out of Orlando into Manchester, rented a stick shift – fortunately I knew how to drive one – and drove myself all the way up to Gleneagles, about four hours away. Oh, and I should also mention that I was driving on the wrong side of the road, sitting on the wrong side of the car, shifting with the wrong hand. I ran into the curb quite a few times!! It was a relief to finally get to the Gleneagles Hotel, one of the only five-star hotels in Scotland.

After a stint with John Redman in 1987-1988, I was back working with my old coach, Bob Toski. The shots over there required finesse and feel, which started to bring back the creative side of shotmaking to my game. Hitting a sand wedge inside of 15 feet was a good shot, not a given, as it was in most Tour events. I ended up finishing T-8, which got me in the British Open! The top five finishers not already in the Open got in. Instead of having to qualify the next two days, I was playing practice rounds at Royal Troon Golf Club!

After rounds of 75-75, I missed the cut at Troon, but I had achieved my goal of playing in my first British Open. My fellow Florida Gator Mark Calcavecchia won his first and only major, in a playoff over Greg Norman and Wayne Grady. It was an improbable win for a couple of reasons. First, Calc's wife was pregnant, and he initially intended to skip the championship to be with her, but she told him to go anyway. And second, the playoff format was four-hole aggregate score, the first time it had been used in that event. The previous format was 18 holes and Calc didn't know it had been changed. That was so Calc.

Calc – I don't think anybody calls him Mark – has had an interesting career. He could go very low. He set PGA Tour records in 1992 (tied for lowest back nine in the Masters, 29), 2001 (28 under in the Phoenix Open) and 2009 (nine consecutive birdies). But a pervasive hook caused him to make some big numbers on holes, until he went to instructor Peter Kostis and learned how to hit a controlled fade. His British Open win was his only major championship, but it was

BOB ROTELLA AND FENDER MUSIC

nearly his second. In the 1988 Masters he was in the clubhouse, tied for the lead with Sandy Lyle when Lyle made his improbable birdie out of a fairway bunker on the 72nd hole to win by one.

One final note about Calc that many people are not aware of or may have forgotten. He inadvertently ignited the "Square Grooves War," which pitted golf's sanctioning bodies, including the PGA Tour and the USGA, against club manufacturers, primarily Karsten Manufacturing, makers of Ping clubs. The shot that set lawyers in motion all over the golf world was a Ping Eye2 8-iron that Calc hit out of the rough on the 16th hole at Eagle Trace on his way to winning the 1987 Honda Classic. He was hitting to a peninsula green, and normally a shot out of the rough would come out with less spin and have little chance of holding the green. Yet this shot not only held, it even sucked back.

Turned out the grooves in his clubface were of a shape – square or u-shaped – that better gripped the ball than the standard v-shaped grooves and thus imparted more spin. Many observers, including Jack Nicklaus and Tom Watson, felt that the new grooves were an example of technology replacing skill, and urged that they be banned, which the USGA did the following year. Inevitably, lawsuits followed, and it ended up being settled out of court. Suffice it to say that subsequent rules limited the effectiveness of grooves, but they're still better than the v-grooves back in 1987.

The square grooves debacle also inspired a Jake Trout and the Flounders song, "Square Grooves" (Are Goin'), sung to the tune of Warren Zevon's "Werewolves of London."

THE JOURNEYMAN

Late in the 1989 season I had my best tournament of the year – a T-4 at the Southern Open. That led to me finishing 117th on the money list and securing my card.

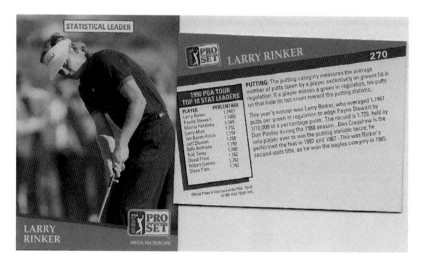

1990: Larry's Pro Set Putting Stat Leader Card

In 1990 I made the top 125 without a top-10, which is hard to do. I had six top-25s, made 18 out of 30 cuts and again finished 117th on the money list. With one week left on the schedule, I was in third place in the putting statistical category. For five years during this period, Epson was the sponsor of the weekly and yearly stats with the winners receiving $25,000. The last tournament was the Tour Championship and I wasn't in. On the Monday after the tournament I went down to see Bob Toski to start working on my game for the offseason. Tuesday morning my wife called and said, "According to the paper you are tied for the putting stat with Payne Stewart." I said, "Call the Tour and see what they say." They took the numbers out to a fourth decimal point and I won by 1/10,000 of a percentage point! That's why I have the license plate 1PUTT.

BOB ROTELLA AND FENDER MUSIC

I found a hand-written note that I wrote in September of 1990.

> I am writing in response to all the trash I keep reading about instruction in today's golf magazines. I'm so tired of hearing "no hands, release the right side, keep the grip of the club pointing at the center of the body," and "the body squares the club at impact."
>
> I have a question. How can so many different grips, swing planes, tempos and set-ups on the PGA Tour produce great results? Try to tell me Lee Trevino is on plane at the top of his backswing, or Raymond Floyd keeps the grip of his club pointing at the center of his body on his backswing, or Lanny Wadkins has "no hands" on the follow through. How can they all be such great shot makers? They know where their arms and hands are going in the golf swing.
>
> It is interesting to read instruction articles that don't relate to the path and clubface angles. They are more interested in the hips, shoulders, and other things that only support a good arm and hand swing. I was taught and firmly believe the arms and hands control the golf swing. The hands control the clubface and the arms control the path. The secret in the golf swing, if there is one, is the proper blending of the arms, hands and wrists. You do not have to think about turning your shoulders, turning your hips, releasing your right side and shifting your weight, if you swing your arms and hands properly. You mean I don't have to think about anything but my arms, hands and wrists? Yes.

THE JOURNEYMAN

How many of you understand the ball-flight laws? Well, you should before you play golf again and start thinking: clubface = hands. Path = arms.

Keep Swingin!
Larry Rinker

I never sent that letter to anyone. I believe it was in response to new teachers doing articles for Golf Digest. Before 1990, it was just the Golf Digest teachers who were doing the Golf Digest Schools that wrote articles. They had a continuity that is nowhere to be found today. Too bad I didn't take my own advice and just work with Bob Toski and these teachers.

At the end of 1990 I founded, managed and operated a charity event in Orlando that would run for eight years, staffed primarily with volunteers. During that time, we had Red Lobster and AT&T as title sponsors along with AAA, American Express and Continental Airlines. We had a pairings party/auction with Outback Steakhouse as the sponsor on Sunday night, with entertainment that included my friend, Rock and Roll Hall of Famer Stephen Stills. On Monday we had a pro-am that included players from both the PGA Tour and the LPGA Tour. We became one of the most successful fund-raising tournaments in the state and raised more than $250,000 for the Second Harvest Food Bank of Central Florida.

I did a pro-am for Freeport McMoRan late in 1990 and got to sit in with "Asleep at the Wheel," a Texas swing band. Working on my new jazz chops, I was able to play through and solo on "All the Things You Are," which is a song every jazz musician cuts their teeth on. Afterwards I got to hang out with the leader, Ray Benson, who said he knew someone at Fender Guitars who was into golf. That person was Dan Smith.

1994 AT&T Rinker Pro-Am: L to R, Stephen Stills, Steve Luciano, Larry

Dan came out to watch me play at the Bob Hope Classic the following year and I ended up getting a personal tour of the Fender plant and the recently started Custom Shop in Corona, California. I saw the body of a Telecaster with two F-holes and I knew I wanted that for putting Fender Guitars and Amps on my MacGregor staff bag. Dan and I would become great friends and we ended up getting several guitars for Tour players. Dan was another one of my guitar mentors.

Chapter 7

Dick Coop and Golf in the Kingdom

DICK COOP AND GOLF IN THE KINGDOM

In 1991 I made the first three cuts of the year on the West Coast before heading home for the birth of our second son, Trevor. We were a growing family and Jan had moved us into a larger house in July all by herself while I was out on the road. Wow, two sons and now Devon had a younger brother.

The day before the Honda Classic started, Trevor at three weeks old was lethargic and the next thing we knew he was in the Neonatal Intensive Care Unit at Broward Health Medical Center. That was a scary night, but it turned out he was OK and was discharged from the hospital after two nights. It was a serious reminder that life even on the road is about more than golf.

After missing the first three cuts in Florida, I asked my father if he thought it was a good idea to go see one of the top Tour teachers, and he said yes. The teacher had recently come out with his first book. As I read over my notes now, it wasn't an upper-core swing.

> Turning of right knee will help getting into right side. Turn everything through together. Don't feel any hit with the hands and arms. Body turn is squaring club and taking club through to the top. Drills, Towel, practice swing no hit with arms and hands.

I went to Hilton Head and shot 77-77 with 26 and 25 putts, respectively. I came home and told this new teacher, "This isn't working." He said, "Larry, you know how to play. Go out and play the

THE JOURNEYMAN

way you know how to play." "You mean forget what you have told me and go play?" "Yes." I went back to playing with my arms, hands and wrists with the feels and shots I learned from Bob Toski.

My confidence was pretty shot. I had just missed four of the last five cuts and had taken two weeks off to sort things out. The next event was the BellSouth Atlanta Classic. I remember hitting a 5-iron into the third hole and thinking wow, that was a great shot. Hadn't felt that in a while. After a 72-67-70-69 I finished T-19. After a tie for fifth at the Buick Classic and making the cut at the U.S. Open at Hazeltine, which my friend Payne Stewart won, I went to see Dr. Dick Coop, a noted sports psychologist who had stayed with Payne the week he won at Hazeltine. Here are some of my notes:

> I already have program. Just need to run it. Don't need more in. Three things. 1) Pick a spot target on the ground, 2) Signal to start routine, 3) Breathe while over the ball.
>
> Trust that going sooner will be better in the long run. Doesn't help to get stuck. Play first three holes on the golf course on practice tee or a hole that I have trouble with.
>
> Feel it more than think it. Be more target orientated as opposed to back swing. Think through the ball more than behind the ball. Play more intuitively rather than analytical.
>
> Get lost in shot making. Let the game come to you.
>
> Need process. Discipline. What's my next shot? How am I going to play it? It's not bad to have a bad thought. Just don't invite it to stay.

Stay in the present, have fun, and be patient. Keep score by the process. Don't be afraid to hit more creative shots.

Once a week play 3 or 4 holes with just a 4-iron. This gets me more into shot making and my right brain.

You can't control the outcome, but you can control the process.

I can run my program and put good move on it every time.

1992. British Open, Muirfield

In 1992 I started the year off with three made cuts and a T-7 at Pebble Beach. I took a week off and went back to see my old coach, Bob Toski. In those days coaches didn't travel the Tour. You had to go see them. I was also continuing to work with Dr. Coop, who said that visualization of the swing behind the ball was helping my flow.

Visualization ties routine to in-body swing. Perspective-Patience-Visualization-Flow equals success.

I liked to walk through the self-help section of bookstores, and now I was reading "Psycho-Cybernetics" by Maxwell Maltz, which was required reading for my brother Laine Jr. when he joined the Brevard golf team in 1972. The next book Coop recommended I read was "The Golfing Mind" by Vivian Saunders. Coop said, "Hang in there. The road to success is always under construction." I was playing decent, had a couple of top-10s and was making most of the cuts. Here are some of the highlights of Vivian's book:

Free mind of fear of failure and game can be

played uninhibited. I'll handle it. Want to feel momentum rather than describe it.

Picture the ball, picture and feel the swing, then execute.

Want to keep mind quiet and work on practiced principles of mental control.

Objective should be to perfect mental strength and abilities and appreciate the inner calmness of the game.

Coop reminded me that the swing didn't start until the top of the swing.

In early June, my wife gave birth to our third child, Morgan Elizabeth. We were hoping for a girl and now we had three children under the age of three and a half. At one point, when Morgan was a little older, we also had two car seats, two strollers, a porta-crib and all sorts of other luggage, so it would take two courtesy cars to pick us up at the airport when we traveled. The highlight of the summer was the tournament in Hartford, where they gave each child a duffel bag full of toys!

1993 Mystic, Conn.: L to R, Jan holding Morgan; Larry, Trevor and Devon

I once again was invited to play in the Scottish Open. The fax, which was from Richard Dorfman, Associate Director of the tournament, read: "After serious consideration both Alan and I (Alan Callan was an executive for Swan Song Records, a label established by Led Zeppelin in 1974.) have decided that what the event needs is yet another guitar player to complete our growing list of prestige musicians. Hence, I am happy to extend an invitation for you to participate in the 1992 Scottish Open Golf Championship at Gleneagles."

For the Scottish Open, I flew into Glasgow and had a courtesy car pick me up and take me to the Gleneagles Hotel. I missed the cut by one shot and now had to travel down to East Lothian to qualify at Luffness New Golf Club for the British Open. I didn't have a rental car or even a reservation where I was going to be staying.

THE JOURNEYMAN

One of the European Tour players' wives told me that the Marine Hotel had a deal for 69 pounds a night for Friday-Sunday, which included breakfast and dinner. We all rode down on a bus that dropped each of us off at our respective hotels. I got in a practice round the next day and prepared for the qualifier.

The wind howled the first round of the qualifier and gusts were over 40 mph. It was a gale! I birdied 15-16-17 coming in to shoot 67, two under. Jay Townsend asked me what I shot, and when I told him he said, "How??" Day 2, the wind howled again, but I chipped in on No. 1, shot 66 and had the low round of the day again. I was in the Open. Now, I didn't have a place to stay that night because the Marine Hotel was fully booked, and the room had tripled in price since Sunday night. My good friend Donnie Hammond had also qualified, and we ended up at the Quarterdeck in North Berwick to celebrate. The owner of the place, Jimmy, found us a two-bedroom condo to stay in for the week right across the street from Muirfield! WLOQ was my favorite jazz station in Winter Park, and since I was the low Open qualifier, Donnie started calling me WLOQ because I had the best score of the four courses that were holding qualifiers.

For the first round I was paired with Paul McGinley, who would later become a successful Ryder Cup captain and win four times on the European Tour. On the first tee, I remember thinking, "As far as God and eternal life is concerned, I've already won all the majors, so relax, go out and have some fun." I got off to a great start, birdieing No. 2 and eagling No. 5 to go 3 under. I would end up shooting 69, three under. Day 2, I shot 68 and was tied for eighth. Donnie had shot 70-65 and was tied for fifth, five strokes behind Nick Faldo. Day 3, I was paired with Jose Maria Olazabal, bogeyed No. 1 but steadied the ship and finished with a 70 to stay in ninth place.

Day 4, I was paired with Ian Woosnam, and the Prince of Wales and about 12 other people were standing 20 feet from my ball in the fairway on the first hole. They wouldn't stop talking. I asked them twice to please be quiet. It shook me up. I couldn't get settled down and lost my focus. Hit my second shot left and started off bogey, bogey. I finally settled down by the third hole and started playing steady the rest of the way in until No. 17, which was a downwind, reachable par-five.

This is where John Cook missed a two-footer for birdie, bogeyed 18 and lost the Championship. I didn't birdie 17, either, hit a poor tee shot on 18 and had to make a five-footer for bogey to shoot 73. I finished T-12. One stroke better was my friend Donnie Hammond, T-5 in a logjam with six other players. Nick Faldo would play the last four holes 2 under to win by a single stroke over John Cook. This is where Faldo famously said to the press, "I'd like to thank you from the heart of my bottom, oh, I mean the bottom of my heart," because they had been riding him of late. Donnie and I ended up back at the Quarterdeck to celebrate our week with Jimmy and some other Tour players who had played well, Steve Pate and Andrew Magee, who tied for fourth.

THE JOURNEYMAN

1993 Disney World Classic: Larry with Donnie Hammond

It was a great trip to Scotland that ended up being my best finish in a major. I remember seeing Lee Trevino at the Marine Hotel the Monday before the Open, and he was impressed that I had made the effort to come over and try to qualify. In my journal I have written down:

> "I liked my composure. My faith in God helped tremendously. It gave me a great perspective all week.
>
> Perspective and patience. Kept working on visualizing what I wanted ball and swing to do.
>
> Kept telling myself to let go of the outcome and put move on it. Run process, can run program every time.
>
> Best composure in this situation that I've ever had. Thanks

God. Need to keep working on letting go of the outcome."

I would finish the year out with a couple more top-15s and end up 94th on the money list. And that was without my winnings from Muirfield, as in those days British Open earnings were not official for the money list.

The AT&T Pebble Beach National Pro-Am is one of my favorite tournaments on Tour. On Wednesday night they have a clambake where all the musicians playing in the tournament put on a concert. In 1985 I played with Glen Campbell in the Hope and he invited me to sit in with him at the last "Crosby" Clambake. I said no thanks, and later watched him walk up on stage and just kill it. What a talent. I got to be his partner in this event a few years later.

Looking back, I wish I had taken advantage of that opportunity, but I learned a valuable lesson a few years later: If you sit in with someone, you'd better know the first song really well. After working on my jazz chops with Steve Luciano, I went to sit in with a local jazz piano trio in Winter Park. The piano player called a tune that I didn't know really well, and instead of passing, I played on it and didn't do very well. They then proceeded to play an uptempo song that I couldn't keep up with. After the song, the piano player leaned over and said, "I think this is a little above you." It was embarrassing, because I had invited my wife and some friends to come down to hear me play. Some of the best lessons in life are painful, but you never forget them.

In 1993 Rudy Gatlin of the Gatlin Brothers was in charge of the Clambake, and Vince Gill invited me to sit in with him. That year

Kenny G was playing for the first time (he would later be my partner here) and the other musicians were Huey Lewis, John Denver, Tommy Smothers and Scott Record. We all got to jam together and take a solo at the end!

1993 AT&T Clambake: L to R, Larry, Scott Record, Tommy Smothers, Huey Lewis, event atendee, Kenny G, Rudy Gatlin, John Denver, Vince Gill

In May, Stephen Stills came to town for a gig. I asked him if I could sit in and he said yes. I got to play through a mini Marshall stack, and he told his roadie to keep my sound clean so I would cut through. I'd get to play on three to four songs including "For What It's Worth." I'd sit in with him six or seven more times throughout the years and learn a lot. "Time is not a magazine," he would say, and he taught me about time and how it's different depending on what genre of music you are playing. He kind of invented the Caribbean rock groove with big back beats like on "Dark Star." Since he taught me the songs, I knew how he wanted me to play them.

DICK COOP AND GOLF IN THE KINGDOM

I was exempt into the British Open because the top 16 from the previous year were in. I played in the Anheuser-Busch Golf Classic the week before and we flew from there to Dulles. When we arrived, Chip Beck realized he didn't have his passport with him. Uh oh! He was trying to convince himself that he could still fly without it! Lanny Wadkins and I just chuckled. Got to love Chip Beck. He's the one that basically said in the Ryder Cup one year, Commitment can overcome technical difficulties! Yes, it can. He got his passport and arrived a couple of days later.

My friend Mark O'Meara invited me to stay with him and Ian Baker-Finch in a house they rented. Steve Bann was over there caddying for Ian, and we had a great time playing practice rounds together among other things. Unfortunately, none of us played that well in the Championship and I missed the cut.

There were some years where I had to play some decent golf coming down the stretch to secure my card. At the Hardees Golf Classic, now known as the John Deere Classic in Moline, Ill., I made the cut with rounds of 69-67, and through six holes I was 3 over for the third round. I birdied two of the last three holes on the front and shot 29 on the back side to pole vault into the top 10. After a 69 on Sunday I finished T-8 and secured my card for another season.

1994 was a poor year. I am not one to blame poor play on anyone or anything other than myself, but I now know that the instructors I worked with (not Toski) were giving me the wrong information for how my swing worked. I am an upper-core player, which basically means I swing the club with my arms, hands and wrists, and the bigger muscles move to support that. The upper-core player

THE JOURNEYMAN

pivots around his front leg, shifts his weight slightly forward, and then the arms, hands and wrists swing the clubhead past the body. I was trying to turn more through the ball, which was the cancer in my golf swing.

Chapter 8

John Daly's First Guitar

JOHN DALY'S FIRST GUITAR

There was a two-day event in Erie, Pa., that a lot of pros liked to play: the Erie Pro-Am Charity Classic at Kahkwa Country Club. I was on a charter flight from Memphis to Erie, talking about music with John Daly. I had one of my Fender guitars with me in the overhead bin, and I got it down and played a few licks for John. He was immediately hooked. The next morning, we went out to buy his first guitar. We had to drive-thru McDonald's, then "let our fingers do the walking" through the Yellow Pages in search of guitar dealers.

The first store we stopped at had a nice used Fender Stratocaster. The Strat is the world's best-selling guitar and rock and roll history. John pulled out his wallet and peeled off six $100 bills. We needed to get a tuner and some cables, so we stopped at another store. Now on the way back to the hotel I see this store on the left and I say, "Let's stop in there." It was an all-Fender guitar store, the owner was just opening up for the day, and there on display was a Custom Shop Stratocaster. If you ever knew JD, you knew he just had to have it. He asked if he could trade the used Strat in and they gave him $400 for it. So John's first guitar was a Custom Shop Fender Stratocaster.

A few weeks later at The International, I gave John his first guitar lesson. When I showed up to his hotel room, he had all these guitar-music books – Eric Clapton Unplugged, The Best of the Eagles, Lynyrd Skynyrd and several others. I taught him the four basic chords in the key of G: C, D, Em and G, and he was on his way.

THE JOURNEYMAN

On the Monday after the Walt Disney World/Oldsmobile Classic, the first-ever VH1 Fairway to Heaven Pro-Am was staged on Disney property. Many musicians and people from the music world were there. Hootie & the Blowfish had just come out with their first album, "Cracked Rear View." There was a party at the Jazz Club at Pleasure Island. I was playing with Vince Gill, Tico Torres and David Bryan of Bon Jovi, Mike Mills from REM, and Payne Stewart. Vince asked me to start the song off. I played a blues riff, but nobody came in. Played another one, same thing. Finally, after my fifth lick, they kicked in! Vince started singing the old Jimmy Rushing/Count Basie classic, "Goin' to Chicago."

1994 VH-1 Fairway to Heaven Disney World L to R Larry, Tico Torres, Vince Gill, Mike Mills, Payne, David Bryan

For the year in 1994 I had one top-25 and made only 10 cuts in 28 starts. I plummeted way down the money list, finishing 192nd.

JOHN DALY'S FIRST GUITAR

I would have to go back to Q-School for the first time since 1983.

My brother Lee had his Tour card for one year in 1984 and lost it. He went on to play the mini-tours in Florida and in 1988 went to work for Jim Gerring at the Muirfield Village Golf Club in Dublin, Ohio. Lee would be an assistant there for five years and get the job in 1992 as the Director of Golf at the Country Club of the North in Dayton, Ohio, a Jack Nicklaus Signature Design. They always liked to groom assistants for upcoming Director of Golf positions at some of Jack's courses such as Muirfield Village and Castle Pines.

When Jack came to open the club in 1993, Lee played 18 holes with him. Afterwards Jack told his people, "I don't know what he's doing here as a club pro; he's too good of a player." That prompted Lee to go to Q-School, where he made it to the finals and got his Nike Tour card for the next year.

Lee played well the next year, especially at the end, and if not for a double bogey on the last hole of the year at Pumpkin Ridge, he would have finished in the top 10 money leaders and graduated to the PGA Tour. So here we both were now at the finals of the PGA Tour Q-School at Grenelefe in Haines City, Fla.

Lee was playing well and made it easily, finishing T-15. I on the other hand fought hard all week but ended up missing by two or three shots. From here on out, Lee for the most part was the better player. I had pretty much had his number up to here, but now he was starting to play some really good golf.

In 1995 the Golf Channel launched in Orlando, and I ended up doing some work for them over the next five years. Sometimes I was on the road for live tournament coverage, but mostly I was in studio as a guest on "Viewer's Forum" with my friends Peter Kessler and golf analyst Mark Lye.

I would be playing the PGA Tour in 1995 out of the past champions/veteran member category, which is at the bottom of the barrel in terms of priority to getting into Tour events. We would fill the fields where a lot of the top players wouldn't play. I managed to get in eight PGA Tour events and 11 Nike Tour events and win just over $20,000 in prize money combined.

As I look through my journal, I keep seeing things like:

- Want arms and hands to lag behind the chest coming into the ball. The arms feel behind the right shoulder all the way past impact. The feel is the turn is squaring the club.

This is lower-core stuff, where you turn and lag, not upper core. I know now that rotation is a face-opener, not a face closer. Holy cow! – no wonder I couldn't find it.

I'm bouncing back and forth between teachers and have notes from Rotella and Coop! A few good ones from Rotella were:

- Fear is an illusion. Confidence is an illusion. We can make them real. A lot of things that work on the practice range don't work on the course. Confidence is the sum of all the thoughts I have about myself.

In June I had Feel is swing the clubhead, while turning the body. That's a mid-core characteristic where the pivot and arm swing match up. Again, not upper core. Coop in August:

JOHN DALY'S FIRST GUITAR

- Shot for shot
- Preshot routine
- Good visualization
- Don't get ahead of yourself
- When I think about score, think process. Make a conscious decision to play more subconscious. Good stuff.

For the year I worked with at least five teachers. I can't even remember what happened at Q-School that year. Obviously didn't make it, so I would be in the same situation in 1996.

1996 Sloppy Joe's downtown Orlando: Larry with John Daly

Before the Bay Hill Invitational, I got a call from Guy Revelle, who owned Sloppy Joe's in downtown Orlando. He wanted me to put a band together and have the players come down and enjoy some food and libations. Steve Luciano put his band Groove Logic together with a three-piece horn section and I invited John Daly to come down and sit in with us. I remember going to John's hotel room to rehearse for the gig. He had four or five Arnold Palmer/Wilson 8802 putters in the corner of his room. That was John. If he liked something, he had to have it in quantity, be it putters, Diet Cokes, or cigarettes. He came down and we rocked the house.

1996 was another poor year. I played in 19 events and made only seven cuts. I started the year off calling Bob Toski and then went down to see him in February. I told Bob I wanted to work only on my forward swing, and I asked him when was the last time that he thought about the backswing. His response: "I can't remember."

I saw another teacher who said to get behind the ball on the back swing and clear with the hips on the down swing. That is lower core! I was so far off. The upper-core player swings the clubhead past the body with the arms, hands and wrists. It would be 20 years before I figured that out.

I started working some with my brother Lee when I would see him out on Tour. Kept in touch with Coop.

- Have about as much conscious thought as the range. Quiet mind in workshop behind the ball. Come out as an athlete.
- Good shooters have no conscience. It's ok to make a mistake by being too loosey goosey, because I'm already making a mistake by not letting it go.
- If you don't let it go, you'll never know. Winning will be because of the process.

JOHN DALY'S FIRST GUITAR

- Grade each shot whether I played it freely or not.

I'm reading self-help books, my Bible, taking notes, doing everything I possibly can to get out of this funk. Then one day I changed my routine. I decided to do the Davis Love III routine. Full practice swing beside the ball and load the feel. Shuffle into the ball, two looks and swing that feel. I shot in the 60s seven rounds in a row! Now I'm starting to play a lot better heading into Q-School.

I would make second stage at Kiva Dunes thanks to a lot of up-and-downs coming down the stretch, and then head to Santa Barbara, Calif., for the finals. The two courses that were used that year were almost 50 miles apart. We would be playing two rounds at Sandpiper Golf Club in Goleta and four rounds at La Purisima in Lompoc.

I started off the Q-School on the 10th tee of Sandpiper, birdie, hole-in-one and then promptly bogeyed No. 12 to settle in. The final round would get rained out and 48-year-old Allen Doyle would be the medalist and go on to have a very successful Senior Tour career. I would graduate from my fourth Q-School along with my old buddy Donnie Hammond.

Chapter 9

On the Road Again, PGA Tour Style

ON THE ROAD AGAIN, PGA TOUR STYLE

Getting back on Tour was a huge relief. I contacted my friend Chris Sullivan of Outback Steakhouse to see if his company would be interested in sponsoring me. He said yes to a deal where I would have their logo on my visor and my bag in exchange for a dining card and bonuses for TV time. That arrangement got off to a very auspicious start. I got an exemption into the Bob Hope, and my visors arrived the day before the first round. Then I went out and shot 63 to take the lead. Pretty cool seeing my picture wearing an Outback Steakhouse visor on the front of USA Today's Sports page. I would shoot 63-68-72-70-66 to tie for ninth. The top-10 finish got me into the Phoenix Open the next week.

With a top-10 at the Hope I had a good reshuffle number heading to the Florida swing. The Q-School graduates get reshuffled four times a year based on their position on the money list: after the West Coast swing, the Masters, the U.S. Open and the PGA.

I got on a little run making cuts heading into New Orleans. After rounds of 65-69 I was in the final group on Saturday with Scott McCarron and Brad Faxon. We teed off No. 10 around 4 p.m. because of all the rain, and play ended up being halted because of darkness after we played the 17th hole. I had a one-shot lead heading into Sunday, but we still had 28 holes to play.

On Sunday morning Faxon blocked his tee shot way right into the 16th fairway. Somehow, he made par and eventually won the tournament. I remember being tied with Faxon or still in the lead heading into the fourth hole. But I made a double bogey, never to recover, and shot 72. After a final-round 73 I finished T-11. I would have another top-10 at Houston, but I missed a lot of cuts, including one stretch of seven in a row. In my journal I see notes from another instructor who I was working with. He said my leg work is terrible. Clear hips and get weight into left heel. Lower body needs to clear more. That's more lower-core stuff. I shot 6 over at the Western Open and I'm thinking it's all mental. No, it's the wrong information for me as an upper-core player.

The AT&T got rained out after two rounds. This was the year of El Niño. To avoid canceling the event altogether, much like 1996, the officials decided to set a resumption date of Aug. 17 to finish the event and make it an official PGA Tour minimum of 54 holes. I got paired with Phil Mickelson and Andrew Magee based on our tee times from February, not the leaderboard, because Phil was one back. Phil had just shot 79 in the final round of the PGA in Seattle the day before.

When Phil first turned pro, we played quite a few practice rounds together. His coach, Dean Reinmuth, was a disciple of Bob Toski. Phil's dominant hand was his right, mine was my left, and we both played the opposite way, so we had a lot of discussion about the role of the lead arm and hand in the golf swing.

There were no leaderboards or grandstands up that day at Pebble Beach. Pros were still playing all three golf courses. I was missing the cut, so it was fun to watch Phil navigate around Pebble Beach. On 18, he hit driver, 2-iron to the back-right portion of the green and two-putted for the victory! He shot 67 after a 79 the day before. That's so Phil.

ON THE ROAD AGAIN, PGA TOUR STYLE

Heading into the final event of the year in Las Vegas, I was bubble boy – No. 125 on the money list. I had just missed the cut at Walt Disney World. Here are some notes from Dick Coop:

- NATO, not attached to outcome, get attached to process.

- Train in practice, trust in competition. Can't train and perform at the same time. Get determined to let go.

In those days the Las Vegas Invitational was a five-round event played on three different courses with amateurs, and the last two rounds were pros only at TPC Summerlin. Steve Wynn used to do a pro-am for the high rollers at Shadow Creek, a golf course designed by Tom Fazio and built by Wynn that opened in 1990. We would have a small purse and then be RF&B (room, food, and beverage) for the week at the Mirage in a suite. I met Steve Wynn's younger brother, Kenn, in 1984 and we struck up a friendship.

I had dinner with Payne Stewart on Tuesday night, and he looked me right in the eye and said, "Are you going to make it?" Meaning the top 125. I said, "Yes I am!" I really believe I made it right then and there. I had just missed the last three cuts, so what made me so confident all of a sudden? Commitment can be stronger than technical difficulties.

My first round was at the Desert Inn and I was paired with Rene Angelil, Celine Dion's husband. He was the nicest man. I was playing well and on our 14th hole, No. 5, Celine Dion showed up to watch. Wow. I played well coming in and opened with a 66.

The second round was at Las Vegas CC and I shot 69 to get to 9 under. The top 70 and ties was at 6 under through two rounds.

THE JOURNEYMAN

Friday morning, cut day, a cold front came through. It was blowing 30 mph and temperatures were in the high 50s. I missed the green at No. 10 but saved par, chipped in on 11 for birdie, and now I was 30 yards from the hole short of the green on 12 for my third shot on the par-four. I hit it to four feet and made another par.

On the front nine it was blowing so hard that my tee shot didn't reach the fairway on No. 6. I had to lay up. Then, from 76 yards, somehow I holed out!! I parred the seventh and the eighth, then bogeyed No. 9 to shoot 75 and make the cut by two. The average score that day was 74. The first two rounds it was 69. I think I hit only five greens that day with 25 putts.

The wind blew again on Saturday and I had the low round with 70. On Sunday I shot 71 to finish T-23 and end up 124 on the money list. I made just 15 cuts out of 33 events. I have in my journal:

- Close to God. Worked on short game. Very Important.

- I learned I can play well when I'm nervous if I get determined and positive. Trusted my swing and stroke.

After the round, Payne and I had dinner, then headed over to the Hard Rock hotel. I remember he was different. He started asking me about my round, and when I said I went for the flagstick out of a bunker on No, 11 and made bogey, he said you could have hit it 40 feet to the right and two-putted from there. I never thought of that. Payne was never one to talk about the golf swing, and hardly ever would ask these kinds of questions. Was he changing? He was, and other people would start to notice and realize it as well.

ON THE ROAD AGAIN, PGA TOUR STYLE

Here's a good trivia question for you: After Tiger Woods' historic 12-shot win at the 1997 Masters, he then won (with his "C" game) the next event he played, the Byron Nelson Classic. Who finished second? The answer: Lee Rinker. My brother would play well for the year and ended up 59th on the money list.

The Fender Musical Instruments Corporation moved its corporate headquarters to the Phoenix suburb of Scottsdale in the early 1990s. My friend Dan Smith, a Fender vice president, would move there in 1997 and I would stay with him for the 1998-1999 Phoenix Opens. I saw where the jazz group, Fourplay, was playing at the Roxie on Tuesday night. I had met keyboard player Bob James at home in Winter Park through a mutual friend, Chris Taylor. Bob was playing in the Monday pro-am at the Phoenix Open and he invited Dan and me to come down to the show.

Fourplay was a super group where all of the musicians had solo careers; Bob James, Lee Ritenour, Nathan East and Harvey Mason. Harvey is a world-renowned drummer who has done session work with everybody from Barbra Streisand to Michael Jackson and was in the Headhunters with Herbie Hancock. We struck up a friendship where a few weeks later Harvey would come out and walk the fairways of Riviera with me in the practice round for the L.A. Open. Harvey loved golf as much as I loved music.

I got off to a decent start in 1998, making five out of the first six cuts. I missed the cut at the Honda and next up was a "home game" at Bay Hill. My brother Lee was staying with me. On Tuesday night I slipped on the stairs and landed right on my tailbone with no brace of the fall. I was hurting. At The Players Championship the next week, I got several cortisone shots before the first round from my old friend Dr. Richard Polisner, who is now living in Ponte Vedra.

On Thursday morning I was playing terribly. Finishing on the front nine, I made a 10-footer for par on No. 8 and a 30-footer for birdie on No. 9, and still shot 78. After eight holes on Friday afternoon, I appeared to be headed for a missed cut. But after I birdied No. 9 and my wife took the kids back to the hotel to try to check out early, I started making a bunch of birdies. When I walked up to the famous island green on the 17th hole after my tee shot found land, guess who was sitting behind the green? My family! They had seen on the computers in the hotel that I was making a run. I parred 17 and 18 to shoot 67 and make my 250th career cut!

1998 Players: Larry with Tiger, Devon, and Brian Mull coming off the 18th green

ON THE ROAD AGAIN, PGA TOUR STYLE

On Saturday I was paired with Tiger Woods. I was exhausted and still hurting, and I don't tend to play well the first time with superstars. Here's what I remember about that round: Tiger was extremely focused, didn't talk much and had an incredible short game. He hadn't figured the course out yet, so he wasn't scoring. Tiger 73. Rinker 81.

I missed nine out of the next 10 cuts. While I was sitting in my hotel room Saturday morning at Quad Cities after missing that last cut, Anthony Robbins came on the TV. He had this new "Personal Power II" program for "Unlimited Success." I had tried everything else, so why not try this? I did this program successfully for the rest of the season. I finished T-12 the next week at CVS and T-20 the following week at the FedEx St. Jude Classic.

Three weeks later, I was at The International in Denver at Castle Pines, and played in the Wednesday pro-am. We played nine holes and then switched groups. While I was waiting for my next group, here came Darius Rucker with two other members of Hootie & the Blowfish. We became immediate friends. I ended up going to their concert at Fiddlers Green that night, getting to go backstage and hang out with the band. They invited me to play in their Monday After the Masters Pro-Am the following year. As for the tournament, I made it to Sunday in the modified Stableford format and finished T-21.

I ended up making nine out of the last 11 cuts heading into the final event, the National Car Rental Classic/Disney. I was 134th on the money list. I shot 69 the first round at the Palm course, but on Friday made a triple bogey on No. 5 to make the turn in 41. Now I needed to shoot 2 under on the back nine to make the cut.

THE JOURNEYMAN

I birdied the par-five 10th and holed a wedge shot for eagle on 13! Now I was one shot inside the cut line. On 18, with water on the right, I played it safe, hitting into the left-hand greenside bunker. I made bogey and made the cut on the number. On Saturday I was even par going into No. 9 and made birdie. Then I shot 4 under on the back for 67. Now, if I played well on Sunday, I had a chance to make the top 125.

I was really nervous standing on the first tee and trying to settle myself down. I barely got the clubhead on the ball and got it in the fairway. My wife ran up to me and said, "You were shaking over that tee shot." I said, "no kidding!" My playing partners were 40 yards in front of me, and I was facing a downwind 5-iron shot into the green. Which I promptly holed for eagle!! That calmed me down. I made the turn and my wife came up to me and said that it would be a nice reward to go to L.A. and record a song with Harvey Mason if I made the top 125. She knows how to motivate me. That would certainly be more fun than going to Q-School.

I got to 18 thinking I needed a par to make it. My tee shot found the right-hand side of the fairway, and it's a 5-iron again. For so many months I've been working on my routine and getting freer. I had been stuck over the ball and had trouble getting the clubhead started. Sometimes my brain would say go and the club wouldn't even move. This time, I stepped up to the ball, ran my routine without hesitation and hit it solid, on the green 20 feet away. Two putts and I'm in! I shot 67-68 on the weekend and vaulted to 120th on the money list.

I did go to L.A. and record that song, "Green Augusta," with Harvey Mason. The song is co-written by Harvey and me and is about

ON THE ROAD AGAIN, PGA TOUR STYLE

my first Masters. I also got to spend some time with my friend Stephen Stills. When I asked him if he wanted to play on the song, he passed, saying, "I've never been to Augusta. Graham (Nash) will do a great job for you." When I got to Harvey's, he asked, "What is Graham Nash going to do?' I said, 'Sing harmony." We were a little alarmed when Graham showed up with stitches in his mouth from some dental surgery, but he proceeded to lay down three harmony parts in about 40 minutes. Now Harvey's tune was "Where did you get this guy?" Graham was the genius of the vocals for Crosby, Stills and Nash.

Chapter 10

1999 and My Friend Payne Stewart

1999 AND MY FRIEND PAYNE STEWART

1999 in Phoenix, I again stayed with my friend Dan Smith from Fender. Robben Ford was playing in town and we got to see his show. Dan was kind of a surrogate father to Robben and designed the "Robben Ford" Fender signature guitar for him. Dan always loved the Gibson 335, so it was basically that guitar with the F-holes covered up, so it wouldn't have as much feedback.

We got to have dinner with the band before the show and I asked Robben about a book of his that I was studying called, "The Blues and Beyond." He said everything is in there that you need to know, which was all kinds of scales and chords for the blues and beyond. Robben is kind of the Nick Faldo of guitar when it comes to precision and playing. He had a devoted following of guitarists who wanted to infuse the genres the way he did, mixing blues, jazz, rock and funk. I have the number "1" prototype Robben Ford Fender. Dan sent it to me unannounced one day. I feel like I have one of his children.

At TPC Scottsdale, Payne Stewart asked me how I was getting to Pebble. I told him that I was flying into San Jose and driving down. He said, "Why don't you fly with me, bud?" I asked him how much it was going to cost, because he had sent some invoices to players who had flown with him before. He said, "I'm not going to charge you, bud." We flew out of Scottsdale with his caddie, Mike Hicks, and landed at Pebble Beach. It was Super Bowl Sunday – Broncos vs. Falcons – and we got to my buddy Geoff Couch's house where I was staying, before halftime.

THE JOURNEYMAN

1999 Fender Guitars: Golfcaster and #1 Robben Ford

Larry's Tour bags

1999 AND MY FRIEND PAYNE STEWART

The phone rang and Payne answered it. The caller said, "Who's this?" to which Payne replied, "Who's this?" "I'm Geoff Couch and you are at my house!" Payne replied, "You better hurry up and get over here. We're drinking all your beer and smoking your cigars!" The three of us ended up going to dinner at Roy's at Spanish Bay where Payne was staying. Payne ran into some guy in the lobby who he didn't even know and invited him to join us for dinner! That was Payne.

We went to the Sardine Factory for dinner on Tuesday night with some more friends including Harvey Mason, who came up to play in the Monday pro-am at Monterey Peninsula for the Boys and Girls Club. Geoff told me that "the sommelier is going to be pulling the clubs tonight," and when he suggested Heitz Martha's Vineyard, Payne said, "We had that the other night. Do you have any Silver Oak?" and they did. We all went back to Geoff's house where he had a little studio and drum kit set up, because he was a pretty good drummer. We jammed, it was a great evening and I had a blast getting to play with Harvey and everyone else.

Payne had won only one tournament since the 1991 U.S. Open and he was finally out of his old club and ball deal. With no bag sponsor, he was so proud of the bag he bought at Edwin Watts in Orlando, and he was back playing a Titleist ball with forged MS-4 Mizuno irons that he got from his old pal Lamar Haynes. Payne would hit it stiff with a 5-iron and birdie No. 18 at Spyglass to take the lead into the fourth round, which would get rained out, meaning he was the winner. In June he would win the U.S. Open at Pinehurst for his third major.

THE JOURNEYMAN

In the winter of 1996, Payne had invited me to a party at his house. When I showed up he handed me an open bottle of Silver Oak and said, "Here, bud, this is for you. Congrats on getting your card back." Three years later, after Payne and five others died in a plane, Mark Wiebe and a group of us drank Silver Oak to honor our friend on the night before Payne's memorial service in Orlando and we continue to do so.

In the spring the local jazz station in Winter Park, WLOQ, hosted an all-star concert in the town of Celebration with Bob James, Larry Carlton and Harvey Mason of the group Fourplay, along with Joe Sample, Kirk Whalum, Chris Botti, Ricky Peterson and others. I got to hang and sit in on the encore. Bob James said he was paying close attention to my solo and wondered what I was thinking. I said, "I'm not going to upstage anyone here, keep it simple, and groove." Three things I learned through the years about sitting in: know how to stay out of the way (don't overplay,) keep time, and solo when you're called on.

PGA Productions was doing a story on brothers on the PGA Tour. Lee and I were included with Brad and Bart Bryant, Danny and David Edwards, and Kurt and Tom Byrum. They arranged for me to sit in with the King B's at BB King's in Memphis. The band said I could play one song and if I did well I could play another. I said, let's do "The Thrill is Gone." My minor blues chops were good, and I got to play a second song. My brother Lee would say in the piece, "Larry's just a frustrated rock musician that has to play golf for a living."

1999 AND MY FRIEND PAYNE STEWART

1999: Larry sitting in with the King B's at BB King's in Memphis

In Hartford, I played a practice round with Paul Azinger. Paul and I met playing the mini-tours, and we spent a lot of time together in the late '80s when I worked with his coach, John Redman who taught at Winter Park Pines less than a mile from my house. When we both hit it in the left bunker on No. 6, I said, "Paul, I'm really struggling with my bunker game." He said, "I can help you." From my journal:

- Play ball off center of chest and get more open
- Get shaft straight up and down and shoulders level
- Release it and keep right shoulder high

Buried lies

- Get closer to ball and on top of it
- Open face get hands back
- Get vertical on backswing and down swing

- Get weight left and right shoulder higher
- Hit down on it, turn the face under and stick it in the ground.

Practice

- Practice a normal lie, normal shot, and normal swing and fly it about 15 yards. Get the feel of the distance and then:
- Hit shots with weight left (goes shorter)
- Hit shots with weight right (goes further)
- Now I have a feel for the distance.

You would think after the finish to 1998, I would have a good year in 1999 but that didn't happen. I missed 16 cuts out of the first 22 events through the Reno-Tahoe Open. I decided to go to Pebble Beach and work with Fred Shoemaker, who wrote the book, "Extraordinary Golf." I studied his book before I arrived and when he filmed me throwing a club, I had the lower-body action I had been seeking for 20 years with my hips rotated like an average Tour player at impact! I began to just feel like I was throwing a club to a target with a square clubface. From my journal:

I have a choice when I hit a ball.

- To swing with the past and worry about being embarrassed or step up and let it go freely.
- Judge shot by process – did I really let it go like my life depended on it? How committed was I?
- Can a person recognize who they are being?
- Great golf never comes out of the past. It comes out of vision. I'm letting go in order to achieve not to simply let go.

- Letting go is being and seeing something without a story.
- Instead of actions, I want to work on the point of view that gives the actions.
- Awareness is reality. Thinking is fantasy. Don't let outcome of last shot mean anything.
- Want to be someone who is present and focused, seeing my future. Creation = future = seeing. Have to give up conscious control to gain control (present.) This is the riding a bike kind of control. Get into being creative without fear of failure.

I made seven of the next eight cuts after Tahoe when our world would change forever on Oct. 25. Payne Stewart along with five others would perish in an out-of-control airplane that crashed into a field in South Dakota. Most experts say the plane lost cabin pressure, and the pilots only had seconds to react before they were all unconscious.

There was a wonderful memorial service for Payne at the First Baptist Church in Orlando, where I am a member now. More than 100 PGA Tour players attended. Vince Gill wrote a song, Michael W. Smith came in on the red eye from Calgary to play two songs, Paul Azinger, Chuck Cook and Tracey Stewart spoke. A couple of my favorite things Payne used to say were, "You've got to have fun, and patience is a virtue." Payne would finish third on the money list for the third time, win three majors, and was third on the all-time money list when we lost him.

I would miss that last cut in Mississippi, the week we lost Payne, finish 187th on the money list and head back to Q-School. My brother Lee finished outside the top 125 for the first time since

THE JOURNEYMAN

he got his card back in 1994 and ended up 173rd. He had just finished 96th, 111th, 59th and 110th on the money list in 1995-1998 with two second-place finishes. We both made it to the finals at Doral and missed getting our cards back. Lee would play the Buy.com Tour and I would bounce back and forth between both tours in the following season.

Chapter 11

Fred Shoemaker, Intention and Commitment

FRED SHOEMAKER, INTENTION AND COMMITMENT

I got a phone call from the Tour office on Monday, Jan. 10, notifying me that I was in the Sony Open in Hawaii. Non-exempt members of the Tour, playing out of the past champion/veteran member category, fill the fields when more players are needed. This year our category would get reshuffled within itself during the year at the same time the successful Q-school and Buy.com graduates were.

I missed the cut in Hawaii and was scheduled to go to see Fred Shoemaker in Pebble Beach on Monday. On Saturday I was sitting in my hotel room watching the telecast and I saw Jesper Parnevik with a 10-foot putt for par on 13. I noticed his energy and thought he's going to make it, which he did. I thought, my energy level was nowhere near that this week. Let's see if Fred can help. From the journal:

- Freedom comes with life. All we can do is give it up.

- We have never been trained in concentration. Great days just come from being in reality. Over controlling – having your mind telling your body what it already knows how to do.

- More present equals more control. There is an intelligence inside me much superior than, "to keep my left arm moving."

- My commitment has been to worry. If I see a shot, I'm committed. Anything else or any thought or conversation about failing is NOT committing.

- Don't leave commitment at impact. I'll know where ball goes, but it will be by awareness, not a judgment. Feeling without the judgment.

- Trust – Either you choose it, or you don't. When I choose to trust I'm saying I have all the resources. When I don't choose it gets chosen for me and that is doubt.

- It's all about intention and commitment. Awareness will develop you. Tell "Mr. Afraid," I'm not committed to you anymore.

- Acceptance is completing the past. Worry is not being fully committed to what I intend.

- The training is to not let thoughts bounce you around. The game is, is my intention and commitment stronger than doubt? My intention is no doubt strong while I'm practicing. Be world class in practice.

- It's OK for mind to be aware of what body is doing. Just don't let mind control. Stay focused and amp up intention.

- Only debrief commitment to my intention. Just accept whatever I get. The source of performance is intent. Want to be automatic to a target. Only I can distract me. Nothing else.

- With presence we get the energy. The target is the leap of faith. Stay with intention for the target. Make sure commitments are clear.

After a few weeks this was starting to kick in and I finished T-18 at the Buy.com Louisiana Open. In the last round I said, "I don't know exactly how things are going to turn out, but I'm looking forward to improvising and reacting and dancing with whatever I'm challenged with."

The next Buy.com event was the Shreveport Open. I shot 64 the first round and had a two-shot lead. After a 68 I still had a two-shot lead. I talked to Fred that night and he said to "spend a lot of time in reality this weekend." I shot 71 on Saturday and was tied for the lead heading into Sunday. I spoke with Fred again. "Can I be bigger than the story? This is the position I want to be in. I'm well trained. Trust your training. Just let the outcome stories go. If I pay attention to the target tomorrow, instead of the outcome, I'll be successful. Get a little clearer before I start my routine." On Sunday I was paired with Kent Jones, who won the tournament. I shot 73 and finished T-5. It was a disappointing finish, leading the tournament all week, but it was my best finish in quite some time.

I'm now starting to play better. T-28, T-12 and T-16 the next three events on the Buy.com Tour heading into Virginia Beach. It's like the old days. I'm driving, not flying, and I've made the last six cuts. At Virginia Beach I shot 73-71-73 and found myself in the middle of the pack. The golf course had five par-fours that were over 480 yards. There was weather coming in, so it was an earlier two-tee start with the middle of the field teeing off first on both nines.

The 10th hole was one of those par-fours and I had to make a five-footer for bogey. I was well aware that my intention and commitment was not where I wanted it to be, so I kept fighting harder on every shot to get there. My focus started getting a little better each hole and I made the turn at 1 under. On No. 5 I holed a 6-iron for eagle, and then birdied the last three holes to shoot 66 and finish

THE JOURNEYMAN

T-5! This goes to show that when you are aware of how well you are intending and committing, you can do something about it. Most people when they hit a poor shot, blame their technique but have no idea how well they intended and committed. From my journal:

- Have to pay attention to what I'm intending. If I'm afraid or thinking about the trouble, I'm not intending to hit the ball at my target. Pay attention to commitment and keep it.

- Intention-conscious mind making a decision to do something.

- Commitment is an action word. During the action of the stroke, which includes contact and the ball rolling all the way to the hole, are you fully committed or are you doubting something? Cannot let contact take away commitment. That is the training..

- You can be fully intentional, fully amped up and stress free.

- Timing is created by target and trust. Develop to be a person connected to a target and being free.

- Fear always follows doubt and most people try to beat fear. It's too late, it's doubt. Have you ever feared anything you didn't doubt?

- Fear comes from doubt and there is no such thing as a fearful situation. The only way you can have fear is doubt.

- Doubt only exists in a conversation. Only way to have doubt is if the conversation sticks with you. With Tiger Woods, the doubt conversation doesn't stick.

FRED SHOEMAKER, INTENTION AND COMMITMENT

I'm now starting to get in Tour events and making most of the cuts. I go out to see Fred in California for more training.

- Only my awareness will develop me. Always things that cause problems are things we don't experience.

- When you can be present to something you've never been present to, it ceases to exist as a problem.

- Being present is watching without judging. Going from zero to ten in awareness is learning something. Zero to one is the hardest, because it finally shows up on the Richter scale. (Awareness)

- It is possible to get on the other side of fear. In Fred's golf schools he tries to create an environment of no judgment or evaluations. If a student finds there's evaluations happening, then they can be sure it's coming from the student and not the coach.

- Anything that I need to remember, I'll remember.

- There is a way to ask yourself questions. There is no way out of a how or why question. It's just "it," the voice in your head talking. Where am I or What am I committed to right now, are much better questions and keep you present.

- Don't ever try to get freer by mind telling body to be freer. Just get into target and make ball go there.

- No drill or tool works. People work. The fact that I have to look at video to experience something, means I haven't experienced it.

- Get into observing without evaluating when I practice

- Spend a couple of days checking out my center. Am I walking with it, driving with it? Am I with it in between shots?

- Center is just below the belly button. Intend to have the time in between shots to be in center. The more I catch myself going up to the head, the more I can stay at my center.

- Most future things are outcome and worry stuff. Most people don't know they are in the future. If you know where you are, you know everything. When I'm in my head, I'm never in balance. When I'm at my center. I'm in balance.

- There is a difference between thinking and being with a target. The being comes first. I have all I need.

- Being gives all the doing. I can never have enough good outcomes to make the security story go away. I'll have this story the rest of my life. It just doesn't have to mean anything. Don't believe it. It's just another story.

- Security comes from God and just being. I can be myself in the blink of an eye from any story. That's coming back to the present and getting connected to the target.

The B.C. Open was the week of my birthday and anniversary, and they are just two days apart. It's always a three-day holiday for me. I had a friend there named John Monaco who had a band, Unplugged "Classic Acoustic." We met out at the golf course one year and he invited me to sit in. I remember this year we played at the No. 5 Restaurant, Binghamton's Quintessential Steakhouse. Some of the players came out and we had a great time playing all of our favorite classic rock music from the '60s and '70s.

A few years later I was playing a pro-am at the Turning Stone Resort Casino owned by the Oneida Indian Nation in Verona, N.Y. We were playing the Atunyote golf course where the B.C. Open would play in a few years. Rain was in the forecast so they asked me if I might be able to play some music. I said I had a friend, John Monaco, in Endicott who could come over just in case they needed a little entertainment. They said great, let's do it. We played only four or five holes, after which we played music for everyone in the clubhouse. Later that evening there was a party at the resort where Kix Brooks, of Brooks and Dunn, and I got to sit in with the Little River Band.

THE JOURNEYMAN

2000: Larry and Kix Brooks sitting in with The Little River Band at Turning Stone in N.Y.

Fred had told me to treat the B.C. Open as a holiday from all the stories and worries in my head and just see how in the present I could play. From my journal:

- Got to get back into being present, doubt and worry can only exist in a conversation. If I'm worried, I'm in a conversation.

- The fear of the outcome sometimes stops us. No one knows why there is a voice in our heads. There is no consciousness in matter.

- The outcome and security stories are the only things that could ever stop me from being myself connected to a target.

- I'm giving my best on every shot. Watch out for the ledger. The good/bad stuff. Stop the accounting.

- Just accept everything and appreciate the process I'm in.

I open up with 71-69-67 heading into Sunday. I get a phone call from Doc Rivers, who lived down the street from me, and is now coaching the NBA's Orlando Magic. He says, "No hoping, just doing!" I then talk to Fred and he says:

- To be prepared for "it." Get a game plan for tomorrow.

- Set a goal for score but on each shot just be connected to a target. Present. Get ready to deflect all the "it" stories.

On Sunday I played well, but hit the wrong club over the green on 18. Left me a tough up-and-down and I missed a five-footer for par to finish T-15. If I had made par, it would have been a top-10. I spoke to Fred two days later.

- In the game of good and bad you can never win. I gave it all I had and interfered on the putt on 18. That's the whole story.

- The interference isn't personal. One of "it's' last stances is "it's going to happen again." It knows how to get me. I can watch a stream go by, but can I watch a stream of thoughts go by? All I can do is let stories go and make "it" stories impersonal.

THE JOURNEYMAN

- I can either be in the story or playing golf, but I can't be in two places. The worry holiday is every day. Have fun. The fun comes before the mental. Just be myself.

- Get lost in playing like I do when I play my guitar. You won't find yourself in the mind. Only in the action.

- I've really seen myself when I get backed into a corner like at Disney or Q-School. There's this kid that comes out occasionally, but that's the real me.

- All my life I've felt like I've had to prove myself. Anybody that has to do that has never met themselves.

- I can always come back to the present in the action.

- Great golfers think, when I finally accomplish winning a major, the "I'm not good enough" story will go away.

- But "it" gets louder, and they get despair because "it" doesn't go away. Curtis Strange, Ian Baker-Finch, and David Duval never won again after their last major.

- Don't feel guilty for not buying into outcome stories. They sell tickets for the drama in golf. I just don't have to be a spectator.

- Most people think assessments are true. After you're done with assessments there's love.

- In order to create, something has to die. My "it."

- All I have to know is what am I committed to.

- Just keep being myself. Be a person who is at peace with life. Be happy.

I ended up shooting 12 rounds in a row under par and 15 rounds in a row of par or better. More from my conversation with Fred:

- Know that I tried my best at all times.

- Realize that I'm developing a relationship with interference and being present to the interference without "it" meaning anything. I don't have to buy into the story that says, "I can't play well when I feel uncomfortable."

- If I don't feel calm (another story) I can still be present to a target. Just ask where's my target.

- Always have the debrief that I gave my best, with everything that I had, and just forgive myself for my mistakes.

- Don't make uncomfortable personal. It's just a story that was passed down to me when I was a kid.

- A friend of Fred's for one month referred to voice as "it" instead of I. Like "it" wants to go to the store, etc. The story gives the uncomfortable feeling.

- Don't say you stink if you don't measure up. Beating yourself up because you're not good enough has never worked.

- People's lives who work are people who appreciate themselves. The whole idea is to be yourself and

THE JOURNEYMAN

then you don't have to remember anything.

- It always comes back to; can I just be present and be with a target without a story and whatever story comes up, it's not important. Prepare tomorrow to catch the stories. The sooner you catch the stories the less energy it takes.

- Trust is something you generate. I think I need evidence to trust my swing. Trust is something in the moment.

- If trust comes out of the past, it will say no you can't.

- You'll never have enough evidence to earn trust. All issues of trust are self-trust.

- Keep trusting and don't worry about technique.

- My interference is doubt. If tonight I can say I trust myself more, then it was a good practice session.

I was first alternate for the Reno-Tahoe Open, sitting at the Orlando airport on Wednesday afternoon for a 4 p.m. flight when the Tour called and said I was in. Luckily, I got an afternoon tee time the next day, so I could get out to the course and get acclimated. I made the cut and sat in with Hootie & the Blowfish on Friday night. After the set, Darius Rucker came up to me and said, "We gave you a double solo tonight and we don't normally do that. I ran over to you in the middle of your solo and I don't normally do that, either, and then you walked it down with us at the end like you've been playing with us for 20 years!" Peter Jacobsen was there that night and he said, "I've never seen you play like that." Just like golfers, musicians have great nights and bad nights. I had a good one.

The Air Canada Championship was my 500th PGA Tour event. I played well the first two days and faltered in the third before an under-par round on Sunday. The following week at the Bell Canadian Open I shot 74 in the morning of the first round and went back to the Piotrowskis' home where I was staying. I had stayed with them since the first time I played in the Canadian Open. Great people and friends.

I started watching the telecast and Tiger was playing. I noticed where his tee shots ended up and what he was hitting into the greens. He had short-iron second shots into the par-five 16th and 18th, and on No. 1, a 485-yard par-four, he hit a driver and a 9-iron that stopped dead. Earlier in the day on the same hole I hit a good drive and a 4-iron that released 30 feet. The Tour was changing. Big power would be coming into the game. Tiger won the event with a miraculous shot on 18, a 6-iron out of the fairway bunker from 218 yards to the back-right hole location! Tiger two-putted for the win and that 6-iron immediately took its place among the greatest shots of his illustrious career.

I missed that cut at the Canadian Open, as well as the rest of the cuts for the year. You would think that with the good tournaments that I had, which were much better than the last time I played out of this category in 1995-1996, I could find "it," but I couldn't. You would think that with all the great mental-game work I did with Fred Shoemaker that I could empower my game even with technical difficulties. I couldn't. I had to go back to Q-School, where I didn't even make it to the finals.

Even though I was working on being less technical, in my timing

THE JOURNEYMAN

I was still trying to lag and rotate. In fact, I thought the longer it took the clubhead to get to the ball, the more rotated my lower body could be at impact. I would find out 15 years later, this is the opposite of how my swing works. No matter how many other good things I was working on, this was the cancer in my formula. A lot of golfers start working on something and hit it better for a while. Then suddenly it stops working and the swing gets out of sync because we get closer to what we are trying to achieve. Therefore, you'll see players sometimes play their best in the middle of a coaching or philosophy change.

Chapter 12

Teaching Career Starts with Ty Tryon

TEACHING CAREER STARTS WITH TY TRYON

I would never again be an exempt player on the PGA Tour. Exempt means tournament winners, top 125, and graduates from the Buy.com Tour and Q-School. I received an exemption for Pebble Beach, so I headed out to compete and spend more time with Fred Shoemaker. I started out thinking, let it go and dance with the target.

Mikhail Baryshnikov was on the practice tee and I remembered a story Fred had told a few days earlier about him. Someone had asked Baryshnikov, when did you become a dancer? He said when he was 15, he went to the ballet and after watching the ballet he became a dancer. Now he realized he would have to work hard and work on technique, but he knew that day he was a dancer. Rich Lerner of the Golf Channel interviewed Baryshnikov the next day and Baryshnikov said ballet was a lot like golf. You have to work on your technique but when you go play, you have to dance!

I opened with a 74 and Fred said:

- Anytime I'm thinking how, it's a head trip.
  Free equals no thought about how.

- Anytime I go inside my head, I have a 90 percent chance of a bad day. Whenever I'm thinking be free, I'm not free. Just be.

- No doing. Just being. It's freedom with the voices, not freedom from the voices.

THE JOURNEYMAN

- My goal is to make it simpler and simpler.

- I will never get rid of the thoughts or voices in my head.

- I think I have to evaluate all the time, or I won't get better.

- It's just "it" saying I'm not good enough. Just choose observation over evaluation, so tomorrow I don't need anything.

- "It" doesn't think if I'm truly with my commitment the outcome will come.

- I haven't separated intention from hoping, caring, wishing, and desiring. When I can separate intention from all the mind trips and dramas, I will be clear.

- Intention is the most powerful force in the universe. I'm either seeing and being or trapped in the stories.

A few weeks later I headed down to south Florida for the Doral qualifier. The night before the qualifier I did an exercise Fred had given me in Pebble Beach. Lay a pencil down and for 30 minutes, try to stand the pencil up with my psychokinetic energy. It may not stand up but don't let it stop my intention.

I remember standing on the 10th tee and having this incredible freedom to my target. There was O.B. left and right and I really felt if I hit it out of bounds it wouldn't ding my commitment. I was paired that day with 16-year-old Ty Tryon. I had the freedom for 15 holes and was 6 under hitting the ball pin high and playing solid golf. The last three holes were scary because all I could do now was mess it up. I parred in and led the qualifying. Ty shot 77. I shot 68-70 the first two rounds at Doral, made the cut, and finished T-63. The official money would help me get in more tournaments later in the year. Here are some notes from my journal:

- Where the ball goes (outcome leading to security stories) has taken away my intention and commitment.

- When I get caught up in the stories, it's hard to intend and commit. Accepting whatever I get (from ball) has helped my intention and commitment.

- Trust God to handle the outcome and accept what I get. Accepting what I get helps me to be present during the shot.

- Don't let whatever the ball does mean anything. Anxiety about where the ball is going to go, pisses on the action of my swing and stroke. This is the story that has been getting me. I just have caught "it" this week and it's clear.

- The next week in the Buy.com Florida Classic in Gainesville I opened with 68-67-70, T-7, and talked to Fred.

- If I use the unattachment to try to get the score, I'm not unattached. Can I be unattached to the outcome?

- Can I play this next 18 holes unattached but intending? Can I be unattached whether I shoot 61 or 81?

- Can I create this unattachment before I get to the first tee? Can I be unattached to the "I'm not ready" story, or whatever interference comes in.

THE JOURNEYMAN

- Get clear and unattached to the next story that comes in. Can I win the commitment tournament if they put a commitment meter on each player?

- Bob Rotella told me at The Players one year that if I won the commitment game that week he would guarantee me a top-10. I believe that's true.

I would shoot 69 on Sunday and finish T-14. Ty Tryon would open-qualify for the Honda the same week and be in the top 15 deep into Saturday and ultimately finish T-39. That was quite a turnaround from the 77 in the Doral qualifier.

Last year I was playing at my home club, Interlachen Country Club. I get to the eighth hole and a hawk flies onto the green and perches right on top of the flagstick. I hit two shots and drove up to the green. The hawk remained on the flagstick. I thought about Payne (maybe this is a sign) and then the hawk flew away. A few hours later I was on the phone with Fred sitting by the old 17th tee and the hawk flew in again and landed 25 yards away from me. Fred said to go check out native Americans and what animal sightings mean to them, so I did. The sighting of birds of prey means to be more observant about life, so I took that as a sign to not miss out on life, don't be lazy, and go do the things you really want to.

On the one-year anniversary of Payne Stewart's passing I stood in my bedroom and said, "Ok Payne, if you are still here show me a sign." I was going out to play Rio Pinar, where my father had taken me to my first PGA Tour event in 1969. When I got on the range, the guy hitting next to me said, "Hey look at that hawk out on the flagstick!" I started hitting some 6-irons at that flagstick, and after I hit a good one, the hawk flew and landed on another flagstick, as if to say, "hit some over here now!"

This prompted me to write the song, "Fly Away (Payne's Song)" because that's what he did. When all the passengers on that plane lost consciousness they just kept right on flying up to heaven. In early 2001, I had contacted Joe Vitale, the drummer for Crosby, Stills and Nash, to help me record the song. It had been months and he was finally ready for me to come do the vocal at his house. I played in the Buy.com Greater Cleveland Open and on Wednesday I drove down to North Canton, Ohio, to see Joe. He had all the tracks done and we did the vocal. I didn't realize it until the next day, but the day I did the vocal, June 13, was the 20th anniversary of Payne and me qualifying for the PGA Tour.

2001: Larry Recording "Fly Away" (Payne's Song) at Joe Vitale's house with Joe and Joe Jr.

THE JOURNEYMAN

The following week in Greenwich, Conn., Payne Stewart was honored with one of golf's most prestigious awards – the Gold Tee Award – by the Metropolitan Golf Writers Association at its 50th National Awards Dinner. I was invited to play Payne's song. It was quite a day. We started off playing Winged Foot, where Arnold Palmer would receive an honorary membership that afternoon. I got to see some of my old friends, Frank Queally and Chris Mara, who had been members there for years.

2001: Larry with Arnold Palmer in the Grill Room at Winged Foot

Arnold Palmer, Gary Player and Barbara Nicklaus were there to receive an award for the Big Three at the dinner. For the Gold Tee Award ceremony, Payne's teenage daughter, Chelsea Stewart, chaperoned by Paul Azinger and Ben Crenshaw, accepted the award for her father. It was the first time she had accepted an award for

Payne. I got to sit next to Jules Alexander on the dais, a couple of chairs from Arnold. Jules was a celebrated golf photographer, best known for his pictures of Ben Hogan. I closed the show and it was quite an evening.

I went home and back to see my old coach Bob Toski. From my journal:

- The rhythm of the golf swing is in your arms which support your hands, and the shoulders support the arms which reduces the effort of the hands and wrists to create speed. When you swing with grace and ease, then your body you do please. If you swing hard and fast, then your swing will never last.

- The golf swing is a measure of time, and to time the golf swing, the tempo of the arms then dictates the tempo of the body. Tempo creates and controls rhythm, (sequence of activity) which is the turning of the body and the shifting of the body while the club is swinging around the body. This in turn creates an action that's controlled to strike the ball squarely toward your line of play (which creates more consistency). If you have an unforced turn, and an unforced shift, the swing feels fluid and effortless. (Cruise Control)

This is actually written in my journal by Bob:

- "Golf is a non-violent game – played violently from within. Brute strength must be replaced by touch.

THE JOURNEYMAN

An ounce of touch is worth a ton of brawn. The little muscles are the sensitive muscles. The big muscles react and support and assist the smaller muscles. They work in harmony. They work to support each other. Neither is trying to dominate, they assist and support each other to create the perfect swing." Signed "BT."

1. The lead arm is controlling the tempo and masters the golf swing. It's the straighter of the two levers.
2. It travels further than the trail arm. It is in front of the trail arm and leads and controls the trail arm.
3. The lead hand and arm is higher than the trail which is bent.

- Therefore, the trail arm is subservient to the lead arm, regardless of how far and fast the trail arm travels. The trail arm and hand work on and around and about the lead arm. Have tempo in the lead arm on back swing and change of direction, then I can move lead arm as fast as I want to, and the club will still square and find its proper path.

- I would run into Ty Tryon a month later at the B.C. Open where Ty would shoot 65 in the first round and finish T-37. His father, Bill, remembered that round with me earlier in the year for the Doral qualifier and asked if I would work with Ty on his putting and short game. I accepted and my teaching career began at $100 an hour. From my journal:

- Whatever I am working on, always know and feel where the target is in your hands. Stop searching and start executing.

TEACHING CAREER STARTS WITH TY TRYON

- There's nothing I "should" be doing. I'm not hitting the ball where I want to because I'm still not convinced that the Zen, flow thing works.

- Commit to what Fred is talking about, because I had a lot more fun and played better. I'm the same guy that shot 62 at Interlachen CC in February for the course record.

On guitar, I would just try anything and be reckless. I used to be reckless in golf. I didn't care if I hit a bad shot. I was fearless about scoring. Nowadays, if I get 2-3 over par, I say I don't have it today. Just cave in. Have to play spontaneously and freely.

Later in the journal after a round at the B.C. Open: I blocked some shots today way right. I'm trying to throw the clubhead into the ball too soon. Lag clubhead from the top and swing left arm left and rotate. No wonder I was blocking it off of the planet with these swing feels. All of those things make the clubface more open at impact and are low-core swing characteristics. Low-core players have strong grips to match that. I could not have been further from what I would later learn about the upper-core swing, which is my natural swing. With all the great mental stuff I was working on, this was completely sabotaging me!

Back in Orlando I started to work with Ty Tryon on his putting, short game and distance wedges. I was still world class from inside of 100 yards and I taught him a lot of what I had learned through the years. We would work and then go out and play. He was working on his full swing with Kevin Smeltz out at Leadbetter's and Kevin was doing a nice job.

THE JOURNEYMAN

Meanwhile I was still trying to play and resurrect my game. Spent some time with Jay Delsing and my brother Lee, but still not the right answers as I look back now at my journal. I went to see Fred three more times in California. Here are some notes from the journal:

- All great spiritual leaders at some point in their life, realize the voice in their head wasn't them. There is no important thought. Once you choose to go, go with flow and intention.

- He who hesitates interferes. Doubt and flow can't exist simultaneously. Want to make golf spontaneous. Make golf like playing other sports and reacting to a target with flow.

- Don't make going sooner with flow a formula. No formula needed. No, oh this works. I work.

- In motion there is less tendency to hesitate. "It" always wants me to play golf out of a conversation. Train to play golf without a conversation, and when "it" throws a thought out about how to do "it," just don't buy into "it" and come back to being spontaneous without hesitation.

- When a student hesitates in Zen training, the monk whacks him. Go with full intention, no stopping. When "it" says I'm not ready, keep going, never stop.

- Aristotle asked Socrates, what's the best way I can develop myself? Socrates said, "practice dying." The identity story dies, the security story dies, the "I'm not good enough" story dies. The "wondering if I'm doing it right" dies. The "I did something wrong" in that swing dies. Let the bad shots die immediately.

- So, when I hit a shot really freely and then "it' says but,…(security story) Just let that security story die. Put a stake in "its" heart! In a crisis situation, people don't pay attention to "it."

- That's who they can be all the time. Extraordinary in the moment. Gladiators used to say before battle, "Strength and Courage!" Everything I can do in the face of "it" I win.

- Step and fall forward. You have to take a step toward fear to make "it" disappear. You really see "it" for what "it" is. "It" is just an illusion of conditioning. All judging is "it." "It" is just a wall that's like a cloud. You just walk right through "it." No rationale will make a dent in "it." I just have to choose.

- People keep looking for the rationale. There won't be any rationale or evidence to get rid of "it." "It" does not live in the present.

- I've been with the target in my head, but not with my body (arms, hands, and wrists). Have an urgency to learn. All the layers of the interference (worry), the security code, etc. is just all interference.

- Any sport with excellence requires a high state of kinesthetic feel, (In-body experience, no judging) enjoying your body moving and experiencing your body.

THE JOURNEYMAN

- Performance is derived from learning. Learning is derived from experiencing. Experiencing is derived from being present. Be present with my swing and then I can learn.

- Whatever happens on this next shot, in sickness or in health, I want to experience the swing and my body in the present.

- Whole focus is on being, not on doing all these things. I can let go of the "will I get it?" story.

- Who am I being and am I aware of who I'm being, so I can come back to being me. Work and train on my being.

- Make the being more important than the story. Being comes before doing.

- When I used to pitch, I was seeing without an outcome. In golf when I see a target, I see some attachment to outcome. I have to trust in my experience in golf. I know. I don't have to pre-see it to do it. (Ping Pong)

- There's a target without attachment. To create unattachment, the area around the target has to be safe. (Range)

- There's a freedom in making the whole course safe. When the whole course is safe, you can pay attention to the experience without attachment.

- Can I be with a target, and wherever the ball goes it's safe vs. being with a target with the course as fearful and scary.

- Being me, vs. being scared. Real freedom comes from when the whole course or range is safe. Now there is no remembrance trying to manage doubt.

- Precision comes out of freedom and awareness, not out of formulas.

- The training is to hear "it" and know you are always safe, and you know the solution is to be free and accepting everything.

- If my intention is freedom, I'll catch everything that is not freedom. When you catch "it" you are already back, unless you make it personal.

- The moment I formularize, I'm in my head again, trying to get rid of the doubt with a formula. Just go back to center. (Safe and God) Just be 24/7 coming back to center.

So, after working with Ty I was scheduled to caddie for him at the Tampa Bay Classic at Innisbrook and the next week in France at the Trophée Lancôme. I asked Ty's dad, Bill, if I could play in the Tuesday morning pro-am at the Island course. He said yes and that we could work in the afternoon. As I'm playing in the pro-am the next morning, my wife calls and tells me that one of the Twin Towers has been hit by a plane! 9/11.

We played a solemn practice round that afternoon with Charles Howell III and you couldn't distinguish who was the better player. David Leadbetter and Gary Gilchrist were following us, and we just said, "Good shot, good shot…" The next day commissioner Tim Finchem canceled the Tampa Bay Classic and we never went to France.

THE JOURNEYMAN

Bill arranged for us to go play in the "SWAT" tournament at Oakmont, which has been played for decades going back at least into the 1930s. It pits a team's best ball of four or five against others in a match-play format where each group plays against every other group in the field. When I flew out of Orlando, I had never seen the airport so desolate. My friend Bob Ford, Oakmont's longtime head pro, would set us up to stay at the Gate House at the front of the property. When we played a practice round, Ty hit wedge into the first three holes and bogeyed every one of them. Oakmont is one tough place and a great U.S. Open venue. The camaraderie was excellent and it's always great to be at Oakmont.

Q-School was coming up. As a Veteran Member I was exempt into second stage right before the finals. Ty Tryon had to go through all three stages. The first would be played at the World Woods Golf Club in Brooksville, Fla. I would be caddying for Ty, so I spent seven hours making a Tour-quality yardage book. I remember asking Ty to chart the second hole at Interlachen, and he had no clue what to do.

We played practice rounds with Sean O'Hair, who would later contact me to work with him, but his dad thought it was too expensive, even though they were spending thousands of dollars chasing Monday qualifiers. Sean O'Hair would go on to be rookie of the year in 2005 and win four events, including his first at the John Deere Classic. I saw Sean at the British Open the next week after his win at the John Deere and said, "I guess you didn't need to work with me. You've done quite alright."

Many people questioned Ty turning professional at 17, but he had deals with Callaway and Target that would pay him a minimum of $1.5 million over the next three years with bonuses if he qualified for the PGA Tour. How do you turn that opportunity down? Even today good college players look for sponsors to chase their dream of playing the PGA Tour. When pro golfers run out of money, they have to go get a job. Ty not only had an incredible sponsorship opportunity, he had time.

Ty played well in the first round. In the second round he started getting on me about the way I was setting the bag down, which is the way my caddie had been setting my bag down for 20 years. He had a new Callaway bag and didn't want the side of the bag with his name on it to get dirty. On the 10th green, after he yelled at me about it for the third time, I ripped into him and said, "You can get as many staff bags as you want!" We didn't talk the rest of the round. On 18, a par-five, he had an up-and-down for birdie, and I thought, I hope he gets it up and down, so he is pleasant when we finish. Then I thought, what am I doing worrying about whether or not he gets this ball up and down or not? This is crazy!

Ty played well in the third round and was leading or very close to the lead. His dad was worried that my enthusiasm might have waned, because I had told him that I was quitting Ty after the tournament. He offered me a $1,000 bonus if Ty won, and he did. When his dad paid me the $3,000 for the week he said, "that's the hardest you've ever worked for $3,000!"

On the ride home I stopped in at a Wendy's and there was Steve Scott with his girlfriend, soon to be his wife. Steve had shot 7 under and missed. I thought, how hard is it to make it now? Second stage was in two weeks at Orange County National and Ty and I would both be competing. Ty's dad called and wished me luck. Ty shot 64 the first round and made it. I missed. At the finals, Ty would shoot 66 in the sixth round to finish T-23. He had his card. I called Ty to congratulate him and he was very appreciative. He would unfortunately get mono the next year and receive a major medical extension to play in 2003.

As I look at my journal at the end of 2001, I would go see two other new teachers that didn't help, and the information wasn't for an upper-core player. I have written down, "I had an illusion about the swing for many years that wasn't true. Hold angle and go left with arms past impact."

With my income deteriorating as I struggled with my golf game, my family was looking for a gift for me. My oldest son, Devon, saw some wine charms in a boutique store for $20 and said, "I can make those." He started "Designs by Devon" and within three weeks he was selling the wine charms on Park Avenue in downtown Winter Park.

Williams-Sonoma said the wine charms were the most sought-after product that Christmas season. I contacted Howard Lester, the CEO of Williams-Sonoma, and arranged for a conference call in regard to selling them nationwide at their stores, which unfortunately didn't happen. Even the gift shop at Donald Trump's Mar-a-Lago purchased from my son.

The next thing I knew, my wife was making belts and embellishing flip-flops with ribbon and selling them all over the country. She even had spirit-wear T-shirts and sweatshirts that she sold to the

TEACHING CAREER STARTS WITH TY TRYON

local high schools. She did extremely well. While I was spinning my wheels, they came along beside me to provide for our family.

Chapter 13

Short Game Guru-XM PGA Tour Radio

My friend Craig Delongy, who owned "John Craig," the finest men's store in Winter Park, asked me to work with his son Brant on his putting. After a while I was getting referrals for other juniors and had built up a reputation as a good short-game coach. I would even drive up to Jacksonville to work with students that my PGA friend, Kirk Jones, set up for me. Overall, however, times were tough. I wasn't winning a whole lot of prize money and I was just getting started with my teaching career.

I would travel to Pebble Beach again and spend time with Fred Shoemaker. I just kept thinking this was a mental thing when it was really a physical thing. I had a virus in my computer about the swing and no matter how well I intended and committed it wasn't going to work. I would have some good rounds, a 65 and two 66s, but only one top-25 on both tours.

I went to see Toski, but I still had this idea (in my own head) that I needed to rotate through the ball, which I now know was killing me. I had a two-way miss going. I could play decent in practice rounds but once the gun went off, I played differently. That's why I kept thinking it was all mental.

A friend of mine owned a restaurant in Winter Park and asked me to put a band together to play some music for a street festival. Thanks to Steve Luciano and my years of having bands for the AT&T Rinker Pro-Am, I had a good list of local musicians I could call. It was so much fun that I said I want to do this again.

THE JOURNEYMAN

1995 AT&T Rinker Pro-Am: Larry with Bob Toski

I would play around town as the Larry Rinker Band in a quartet with a piano, bass and drums behind me. No rehearsals and I provided charts for all the musicians. Nothing better than honing your chops playing out, the same as playing in golf tournaments.

One gig at Dexter's in Winter Park, I couldn't get my usual sound guy, so I had to go out and buy a new mixing board. Then my bass player had someone sub for him, and my drummer couldn't do the gig. I jokingly asked Harvey Mason if he could do the gig and he recommended his 16-year-old cousin, Emmanuel Dominick, who lived in Holly Hill. I'm thinking, there is no way a 16-year-old can cover everything from jazz standards to Pat Metheny to classic rock. But Manny shows up and proceeds to do a great job. I ask the bass player after the gig, how'd the kid do? He said he was one of the best drummers that he had ever played with.

Manny would play with us again before going off to Los Angeles to study at the Musicians Institute College of Contemporary Music. He currently lives in L.A. and is professionally known as "MannYthedrummer." I would play 25-30 gigs around Central Florida through 2006 including the Winter Park Art Festival.

I would make my last cut on the PGA Tour in September at the Tampa Bay Classic, where a year earlier I was supposed to caddie for Ty Tryon. I remember being Houdini, getting the ball up and down coming in to make the cut on the number, and then finish, as they say, DFL. I was starting to play less and less every year.

I would work some for the USA Network in 2003 covering the Senior Tour and the PGA Tour. In 2003 I played in just three Tour events and 15 on the now-titled Korn Ferry Tour with little success. In 2004 after I averaged 76 for three Korn Ferry Tour events, my wife said, "I think it's time for you to do something else." I had gotten my real estate license the past November and started working in real estate at Coldwell Banker in downtown Winter Park.

THE JOURNEYMAN

One morning I ran into Mark O'Meara at Einstein's Bagels in the Dr. Phillips area near my new real estate office at Masters Realty co-owned by Bill Tryon. Mark and I started talking about what it takes to be a good player. He said, "You've got to putt, you've got to have a short game, you have to be good at hitting the ball pin high, and you have to have a golf swing." I was teaching putting, short game and distance wedges at the time and started to send emails to my students on what we had worked on. After I realized I was sending a lot of the same material, I started copying and pasting things into Microsoft Word. Next thing I knew I had three pages, and this would eventually be the start of a book that I would first publish in 2009, "Rinker's Five Fundamentals." I added golf swing and course management to round out the five fundamentals.

For many years, the only time my children played golf was when I took them out. With my two sons we started off playing par-threes from the red tees, par-fours from 150 yards, and par-fives from 200 yards. One summer in the late 1990s a friend gave us an Explorer van to take out on the road for seven weeks. Morgan proved to be very social, getting to know everyone at the tournaments. She knew everybody's name, and no one was a stranger to her.

After the boys played their first par-three course in Memphis, they got more interested in golf. At the end of that year, we got to team up and compete in the Disney Parent/Child Tournament. I marked my ball with a quarter, then-5-year-old Morgan picked it up and said, "Daddy, look what I found!"

The boys started playing lacrosse in seventh and eighth grade and now they were playing in high school. Spending a lot more time at home, I had time to take the boys out to play golf. We had many fun John Mayer "bump sessions" – getting totally into the music – while driving out to Grand Cypress, stopping at Burger King and getting some lemonade Slushies.

Some of my boys' lacrosse friends were members at Interlachen Country Club and the next thing I knew they were playing every day around Christmas. I always wondered if they would get the golf bug and they did! Then the bill came at the end of the month from the club and it was $2,000! I told them they had to calm the lunches down and then I figured out what they were up to. Texas Hold'em was popular so if it rained, they were inside playing cards, and if it was nice out they were playing golf. Yes, of course they were gambling!

When it came time to qualify for the high school golf team in the fall of 2005, Devon, unbeknownst to me, grabbed a 60-degree wedge with only 4 degrees of bounce out of the garage. Even I couldn't use that wedge. He was in good shape to make the team until he hit it into a bunker with new sand. Normally he was a very good bunker player, but the lack of bounce on this wedge caused the clubhead to go right under the ball. It took him five swings to get it out. On the last hole, he thought he had missed the team so he picked up his ball a foot away from the cup. He could have made it and got in a playoff. Meanwhile, Trevor made the team.

Devon was devastated. He worked hard, and easily made the team his senior year.

From infancy, Morgan was always out for a good time in whatever she did. In golf she would go run and play in the sprinklers when they came on. As she grew, she became very athletic. With very little effort she did well in a myriad of sports including travel volleyball, along with high school golf, lacrosse, water polo, and swim team. Jan was a competitive water skier and taught all the kids how to ski and later compete nationally. Morgan finished second in the nationals when she was 12.

In 2007, I hadn't played a lot in the last three years, but I was turning 50 in July and thought I might make a run for the PGA Tour Champions. Thanks to qualifying through the North Florida PGA Section, I would play in my 525th and final PGA Tour event at the Tampa Bay Classic. I had a friend, Steve Kropp, caddie for me in the practice round and he ended up offering to sponsor me for a crack at the Senior Tour.

Stephen Stills came to Florida on a solo tour and I went over to the King's Center in Melbourne hoping to sit in. Right before he walked on stage, he said, "Come play on something." The second song was "Different Man," which he had written recently when I was at his house in L.A. I actually had recorded a harmony part with Joe Vitale as tech at Stephen's home studio in January for a new solo record, "Man Alive."

So, when Stephen started the song, I walked out on stage and sang the harmony part starting on the second verse. It was only in his monitor at first. Rance Caldwell was wondering who in the heck just walked on stage? Rance had run monitors for Crosby, Stills and Nash for years and this was his home base and venue. I finally was put in the house feed and Stephen credited me with helping him to write the song. As fate would have it, Stephen invited his old pal

Neil Young to play and sing on his new solo record, and this is the song he picked! Yes, I got bumped off the record by Neil Young.

I would end up playing on "For What It's Worth" that night, and when I saw the rest of the set list, I just kept on playing because I knew all the songs. After the gig Stephen's manager came up to me and said, "Hey, why don't you join us in Jacksonville in a couple of days?" In Jacksonville I got to do sound check at the historic Florida Theatre, be introduced on "Different Man," and play on the same songs at the end. After the gig my friend John McGough said to Stephen, "Hey, how about Rinker? He played pretty good tonight," to which Stephen responded, "Yeah, he finally didn't overplay!"

In the spring, I got into two Korn Ferry events where each of my sons caddied for me. The first was the BMW Charity Pro-Am at the Cliffs. My oldest son, Devon, was on the bag and on a par-three on the back nine, I blocked a 4-iron way to the right in a penalty area that was marshy with tall grass. I said, "Devon, let's go look for that." He said, "I'm not going in there," so I said, "Give me my sand wedge."

At the Knoxville Open, Trevor caddied for me. The fifth hole at Fox Den was a bowling-alley par-five with O.B. on both sides. After two tee shots down the right side, we walked down to see if either of them were in bounds, and both were out. I said to Trevor, "Give me a sleeve of balls and my 5-iron. Hopefully I can get one of these in," as I started to walk back to the tee.

In the fall of 2007, I got my broker's license in real estate and started "Rinker Real Estate," on Dec. 31, 2007. I also worked my first event for XM PGA Tour Radio and started to cover the PGA Tour in 2008 as an on-course commentator and as an analyst. I would chase the PGA Tour Champions through March of 2008 and end up getting in only a couple of events.

Let's see. I had four jobs – playing, commentating, teaching and real estate, which was crashing and would continue to fall. Now I only had three, because the playing career was all but over. I would try a few more Mondays on the PGA Tour Champions, but with no success.

I was enjoying working for XM PGA Tour Radio covering the Tour. I finally had someone who took an interest in developing me. That would be Chris Castleberry, who hired me. He was tough on me, had me go take voice lessons. I was working about two weeks a month, so that left time to teach and work in real estate.

Chapter 14

Riomar, Red Sky and Rinker's Golf Tips

For a few years, I had been searching for a position as Director of Golf, but had not been successful. Looking for advice, I called my old friend Bob Ford. In addition to his regular gigs as head pro at both Seminole (winter) in Florida and Oakmont (spring through fall) in Pennsylvania, Bob had started a professional golf services company, AMF, with Steve Archer and Bob Mulcahy. AMF's mission was to help PGA professionals network, improve their business templates and résumés, and, most important, find jobs. Bob told me that if I had been looking 10 years ago, I would have found something. But now everybody was looking for real experience in the golf industry. All I had was that I parked carts and picked the range in high school.

My wife recommended that I look into getting an assistant-pro job to get some work experience on my résumé. She used to tell our kids, "It doesn't matter what you do, just do something; it always leads to the next thing." I looked and looked on PGA Links on the PGA of America's website, and one day I noticed an opportunity at Riomar Country Club, a private facility in Vero Beach, Fla. I had been to Vero Beach 50 times and never heard of this place, and it was right on the ocean. I applied and got the job. I would work the season, November-April.

My first day was Nov. 13. I didn't even have a place to stay. My fallback was my parents, who lived 50 minutes away in Stuart. I asked the Riomar head pro if he knew of anyone who might have a garage apartment or something similar. He said he'd look into it. I stayed at my parents' place that night and went to work the next day. From my journal:

- The staff and membership has been wonderful. Everybody has been so nice. I prayed that God would help me find a place to stay and He did. Alice and Wally Cole, a very nice couple, were so gracious in letting me stay in their mother's home for the next six weeks. It's only 400 yards from the clubhouse and on a really cool street named Sandfly. I'm 300-400 yards from the ocean. I'm very blessed and God has met and exceeded my needs.

Riomar Country Club was established in 1919, the same year that Pebble Beach and Seminole, two of America's greatest courses, opened as well on opposite coasts. Many of Riomar's members were graduates of Harvard, Yale and Princeton. When I started it was a small club with just two professionals, a golf shop manager and three outside service personnel. There were no tee times, and the whole front nine was on the ocean.

I was making $600 a week and keeping 100 percent of my lesson fees – $100 an hour for members, $150 for nonmembers – working six days a week. They asked me to come into the office and fill out some forms. When I looked puzzled at the W-2 form the secretary said, "You've never filled one of these out before, have you?" I said, "No, I don't think so."

I was off on Mondays, but I could teach if I wanted to. I did well with the lessons, so things were working out. I could do an hour-long putting lesson or an hour-long short-game lesson, but a full-swing lesson before I got here was only about 5-10 minutes. I was a short-game coach who still hadn't figured out his own golf swing. I was teaching on the back of the range with no camera, no technology, and nothing but my intuition and experience.

The house in which I was staying was available only for six weeks, so I needed to line up a replacement. A couple I had become friendly with, Dick and Phyllis Dillon, had a garage apartment right on the ocean. They were kind enough to let me stay there, which I did for the rest of my time at Riomar. They were the best. They treated me like family, and we became great friends.

In 2009 the satellite radio company Sirius merged with its competitor, XM. The trickle-down effect on me was not good. I was in the bag room when Chris Castleberry, Program Director of PGA Tour Radio, called me. "Are you sitting down?" he asked. I wasn't, but I said yes anyway. (Does anybody ever say no?) He proceeded to tell me that my salary was being cut more than 50 percent by the new SiriusXM. Needless to say I was disappointed, but I didn't have anything else and it was great exposure, so I said OK. I went back on the air once I finished at Riomar on April 30.

I was still looking for work. One day I was talking to Dick Dillon and telling him that AMF, Bob Ford's group, had a teaching division that I was thinking of joining. Dick was a pioneering advertising executive and entrepreneur. He created one of the first advertising agencies in the U.S. that focused on marketing to Hispanics. He was known for always wearing a pink shirt and was quite the character.

"I can't believe that you are not a member (of AMF) already," Dick said. I joined AMF, and it didn't take long for that move to pay dividends. Shortly before Christmas, I got a call from Lorin Anderson, who ran AMF's teaching division, to tell me that there was an opportunity in Vail, Colo.

The position was Director of Instruction at Red Sky Golf Club. I interviewed for it in January 2010 at the PGA Merchandise Show with Jeff Hanson, Red Sky's Director of Golf. Over dinner, Jeff said, "Tell me something about you that I don't know?" "I'm one of only four players," I said, "to play in at least 500 tournaments on the PGA Tour without a win." Jeff appreciated my candor. In subsequent years he would tell this story many times, always closing with "I like this guy." Needless to say, I got the job!

2014: Larry with Jeff Hanson and Darius Rucker in Vail, Colo.

RIOMAR, RED SKY AND RINKER'S GOLF TIPS

One of the downsides of living in Florida is the damage you can do to your skin if you're not careful about exposure to the sun. In 2010 I had 30 different skin cancers cut, burned, or scraped off of my body with two melanoma in situ (first stage). After one of the surgeries on Tax Day, April 15, I sat in with Stephen Stills at the House of Blues at Disney Springs and got to play on at least a half-dozen songs. It was a great evening. I remember somehow carrying my amp back to the car after the gig. We had Joe Vitale on drums, Todd Caldwell on keyboards and Kenny Passarelli on bass. Stephen had just come out with another solo album, "Live at Shepherd's Bush" in 2009.

In late May my family packed up the Chevy Suburban and headed for Vail. We had never been there before but had some friends who were going to let us stay in their condo in Beaver Creek for a month. Then we would rent a three-bedroom apartment through Sept. 15 at Riverwalk. Red Sky has 36 holes with Tom Fazio- and Greg Norman-designed golf courses, and the Red Sky Golf Academy was located at the end of the range at the Fazio course. Chuck Cook had been the Director of Instruction for the first two years, followed by David Leadbetter for five years.

My first two-day golf school consisted of three people, and when it was over they gave me an extremely generous tip. We needed new tires on the Suburban and the tip was the exact amount of the new tires! Divine intervention. My two children with us got summer jobs and we had an incredible summer.

Getting the Director of Instruction position at Red Sky would change my life forever, and now my career path had switched to teaching. With the commitments I had with Riomar and Red Sky, I couldn't cover the PGA Tour anymore for SiriusXM.

During my first season at Red Sky, I met Pat Hamill, who founded Oakwood Homes in 1991 in Denver. He was a fun-loving guy who took some lessons and would invite us over to "the cabin" for cookouts. Toward the end of the summer there was a cookout, and he asked my wife and I what we were doing. We said we were spending a couple of extra weeks and staying at the Hyatt in Beaver Creek, "Why don't you stay here?" he said. My wife and I looked at each other and thought, the hotel room or the cabin? We'll take the cabin. Before we left he said, "When you come back next summer, just stay here." We couldn't believe it. Pat is the most generous person I have ever met, and we would become close friends.

In the fall of 2011, I went to a seminar that AMF/Proponent Group held at Grand Cypress with Fred Griffin as the host. David Leadbetter presented the 20 things that he had learned as a golf instructor. One of the things was "Buy your own equipment." Up to this point I didn't have a camera, but I went out and purchased one the following week and set up a Branded Academy at V1 Sports. Now instead of sending email reviews, I could send a video with voice-over. I also found out what I really was doing in my swing, not what I thought I was. Tour players are notorious for telling you what they think they do, not what they really do.

I would work at Riomar through the 2011-2012 season, then I set up shop in Orlando at the Core Golf Academy at Orange County National thanks to Sean Foley. Sean helped me to get in touch with the staff at Core and I had an opportunity to be their short-game coach.

RIOMAR, RED SKY AND RINKER'S GOLF TIPS

At Core I met James Leitz, David Orr and James Sieckmann as well as Sean Foley. These four would have a huge influence in my beliefs about teaching going forward. James would teach me how to use Trackman. David would give me some new material for my putting lessons, and James would do the same for short game. Sean would let me shadow him when he taught. The best thing about these three years at Core was becoming friends with and learning from these gentlemen.

In the summer of 2013, I got a call from Michael Pinkey with Trackman, a launch monitor company. He wanted to come show it to me at Red Sky. After a few swings he said that I was swinging too far left. I thought, I don't swing too far left, I swing too far to the right. He said, square up your shoulders and swing more in to out. I did and after four or five more balls he said that was better.

The next day I went out to the range and put some alignment sticks down. I had forgotten that I could sight my left shoulder to see where I was lined up and when I was square, I felt like I was aiming 30 feet right of the target. After about 20 minutes, I started acclimating and feeling like I was aimed correctly.

To me, this is where I stopped trying to turn through the ball on the forward swing. I was a "turnaholic" for such a long time trying to lag and rotate. Now I wasn't and I started playing some better golf. My friend Pat Hamill and I would win the Castle Pines Member-Pro.

In the 2013-2014 season I was teaching in Vail from June through September, in Orlando from October through May and a couple of times a month in Vero Beach thanks to Mark Cammarene, the Director of Golf at Pointe West. I got a call in the fall of 2013 from SiriusXM. They said the channel was expanding and had Hank Haney, Jim McLean and David Leadbetter lined up to do instructional shows, and wanted me to do one, too. Wow. You're putting me in with that group? Rinker's Golf Tips was born.

2018 PGA Show SiriusXM Teacher's Town Hall: L to R, Suzy Whaley, Debbie Doniger, Hank Haney, Jim Mclean, Michael Breed, Larry and David Leadbetter

When I auditioned, I asked if I could get a copy of the show. They said sure because it's going to be live on the air! I knew radio and had been trained by Chris Castleberry. We would have lists of the do's and don'ts for the PGA Tour broadcasts. They didn't want you to pause. This is radio; dead air is bad. Also, be as descriptive as you can possibly be, because your listeners can't see the action.

I wrote out the whole first segment and read it. It was tough going. I had no one to talk to or throw it to for 11 minutes. At the break the producer asked me if I was OK. I said yes and the next segment went more smoothly. At the bottom of the hour I had my first guest on, and from there I was on my way. It was my show and they basically gave me free rein to do what I wanted. I started having guests on every show. I learned a lot, and that made things a lot easier and more entertaining. The first two years my show was on Sundays and then it moved to Saturday and Sundays 9-10 am ET.

Chapter 15

Finding the Wright Balance

FINDING THE WRIGHT BALANCE

In the fall of 2014, I cold-called the Director of Golf, Nathan Stith, at The Ritz-Carlton Golf Club in Orlando. He said they wanted to go in a different direction and would like to have someone there who felt more like a part of their team. I talked with the sales manager, Steve Ousley, at the PNC Father/Son and he seemed to be on board. I interviewed with Nathan in January of 2015 and he created the Director of Instruction position for me to start Feb. 23.

I learned a valuable lesson here. No today does not mean no tomorrow. I had applied here eight years ago. They went with PGA Tour Academy because they had a better web presence. God had blessed me again. His timing, not mine.

A few weeks after I started, I was on the back of the range when Ernie Els rolled up in a cart with his caddie. We said hello, started chatting, and I ended up giving him a putting lesson. He had just missed the cut in his last four events. At Bay Hill, he shot 71 in the first round and then on Friday, holed a bunker shot on No. 9 to shoot 67. After the round he told the press that I had helped him with his putting. Ernie came up to me and asked what I was doing that afternoon and I said I had a lesson from 3 to 4. He said great, I'll see you at 4. We worked on his putting and short game and Ernie had a nice weekend with a 68 on Sunday to finish T-13.

I then got invited to go down to his house in Jupiter, Fla., and work with him down there at The Bear's Club. We would work on his putting and short game and then have contests. He made the cut at Houston and then shot 67 in the first round of the Masters and finished T-22. I would get together with him a couple more times before I headed out to Colorado for the summer.

2015: Larry with Ernie Els at The Bear's Club

I would finish the season at The Ritz-Carlton before getting a two-year contract. When I told Nathan that I could work here year-round he said, "I like it that you go somewhere else in the summer." He was smart. He knew it would be advantageous for me to be the Director of Instruction at two great clubs and catch both seasons.

My business was steady in Colorado, and at the end of the summer I invited the new worship leader at The Vail Church, Nick Carleton, over to the cabin with his family for dinner. He knew me only as a golfer, and I asked him, "How good is your golf game? Can you shoot 75?" He responded with, "No, I'm not that good.

FINDING THE WRIGHT BALANCE

Me shooting 75 is like you being a professional musician." I said, "I am." There was a long pause. He just looked at me as if to say, "Rinker, do you even own an instrument?"

We talked about music at dinner and how we both loved John Mayer. After dinner, I got the guitar out and started playing "No Such Thing," off of Mayer's first album, while Nick sang. I played some more John Mayer tunes and Nick said, "You've passed the audition." I've been playing lead guitar at The Vail Church ever since and we've been able to play out at some country clubs as well.

Nick Carleton and Larry at the Vail Church

I was still building my business in Orlando. In the fall of 2015, I asked someone at church, Rey Ortiz, with whom I had played music at First Baptist Orlando, if he could help me with an IT issue I was having. The next thing I knew, Rey was creating logos and updating my website, and I had an IT partner to help me with all things online. He was also a professional photographer.

THE JOURNEYMAN

Larry with Dr. David Wright

There are teachers who teach the same thing to everyone who walks through their door, and there are teachers who work with what people have. I'm the latter type, and one of my favorite things I've heard is if you have fast hips, don't slow them down, and if you have slow hips, don't speed them up. I had been trying to speed up my hips for way too long. I was now starting to play golf again with my arms, hands, and wrists and letting my lower body move naturally.

Wright Balance

In January of 2016, I would meet Dr. David Wright. I got measured and he told me I was a "9" or upper core. I didn't have any clue what that meant, and I went back to teaching and playing the way I had. My sister Laurie said that she really liked Dr. Wright's material and that I should look into it more.

FINDING THE WRIGHT BALANCE

One Sunday in Colorado, I got a legal notepad out and started identifying the characteristics of the upper-, mid-, and low-core swings. Doc had three swing models: upper-, mid- and low-core, with set-up and swing characteristics for each core region. Doc had ebooks that were 200 pages long. I wanted to get and understand the Cliffs Notes version on the three swing models. When I realized what the upper-core swing was, I found my picture next to it in the dictionary.

The two main ingredients of the upper-core swing are, pivot around the front side of your body, and swing the clubhead past your chest. This was the opposite of what I had been trying to do for so many years. The mid-core swing or average Tour player swing is what most of the teachers I had worked with were trying to get me to do by rotating my lower body more. Adam Scott, Ernie Els, Grant Waite, Steve Elkington, Tom Purtzer ... name your favorite mid-core Tour player that has their hips rotated about 45 degrees at impact.

Low-core players have the strongest grip and are the most rotated at impact. Dustin Johnson, David Duval, Paul Azinger and Lee Trevino. Upper-core players have the weakest grip and their hips are rotated less than 30 degrees at impact. Once I figured out the characteristics of each model, I now understood how all these different Tour player swings worked.

In 2003-2007, Doc Wright set up the research design, wrote the protocols and ran the balance study for the duration of a research project with Dr. Frank Jobe, who is best known for the "Tommy John" surgery that saved the careers of many athletes. Dr. Jobe was intimately involved in meetings planning this balance research. He provided his biomechanics lab and biomechanics staff for the project.

THE JOURNEYMAN

Coincidentally, in the mid 1980s when we first had a fitness center truck rolling on the PGA Tour with physical therapists, bikes and light weights, Dr. Jobe was our orthopedist. Deane Beman said, "I'm more convinced than ever that it's the best thing to come along for the PGA Tour since I've been commissioner." The fitness center was housed in an oversized, custom 45-foot trailer which expanded on each side to a width of seventeen and a half feet.

Also joining the research team was Dr. Michael Mellman, who has been the team physician for the Los Angeles Rams, Kings, Dodgers and Lakers. He has championship rings with each of these teams.

Dr. Robert Watkins also joined the team, and he has treated numerous professional athletes. He is the spine surgeon/consultant to the PGA Tour and University of Southern California athletics. He did NFL quarterback Peyton Manning's neck surgeries and NBA player Dwight Howard's back. His clients include Troy Aikman, Wayne Gretzky, Don Mattingly, Joe Montana and many more. Many consider Dr. Watkins the "Father of Core Training."

Dr. James Smith also joined the team. He has been a research physicist for more than 30 years, receiving a variety of professional awards. He continues to work with Dr. Wright on the stance width and grip size formulas for all sports and activities that require balance applications.

Dr. David Wright has two doctorates. His areas of specialization are research, learning and psychophysiology. He was a full-time member of the faculty of the University of Southern California School of Medicine for four years and a member of the clinical faculty for more than 30 years. He has also been a PGA golf professional for almost 30 years.

FINDING THE WRIGHT BALANCE

With Wright Balance there is a measuring system to determine if you are an upper-, mid- or low-core player. They can actually do it without even seeing your swing. It's based on where you have strength and balance, and the best indicator today is external shoulder rotation. In the measuring they get height, weight, shoe size, shoulder width and sternum width and put all that into an algorithm. It then spits out nine stance widths for the core regions. 1-2-3 low core, 4-5-6 mid core, 7-8-9 upper core. Where you have the most strength is your dominant core region.

I started measuring some friends and pros in June of 2016 and by July, I was ready to start screening my students. I wrote down their stance widths and dominant core region so that when they came back, I could reference it, never realizing that at some point I would start to see what percentage of my students were upper, mid, or low core.

After one year I had 66 percent upper core, 29 percent mid core and 5 percent low core, which most likely is the national average for men. I was starting to see that most of my students were upper-core like me, and we were now able to measure their hands to determine the grip size for both of their hands. In the next few months, with most of my students being 45 and over, more and more were testing upper core.

Jack Nicklaus said it best. He tried to keep his back at the target as long as he could on the downswing and felt like he was releasing the club right away from the top. He said it gave him room to swing his arms. These are all upper-core traits.

In March of 2017, I would publish "Rinkers' 5 Fundamentals, 3rd

THE JOURNEYMAN

Edition," an interactive ebook with 11 video lessons. The five fundamentals are putting, short game, distance wedges, golf swing and course management, with two appendixes: Mental Weapons and Goal Setting. My friend Rey Ortiz helped with the design, and I had some things I wanted to update.

In December, I was pleasantly surprised when Rick Peckham came to work with me. Rick is an incredible guitar player and guitar professor at the Berklee College of Music. We hit it off right away. I got to take two online courses at Berklee, thanks to Rick: Chords 101 and Chords 201, which he taught. Rick has become another one of my guitar mentors.

By the end of 2017, about 75 percent of my students had measured upper core. One day in late February of 2018, I thought, "I have a book right here in my head. I know the chapters and everything." "The Upper Core Swing," The New Revolution ebook with six video lessons was published in April and released the week after the Masters. At the time of the release, I was up to 78 percent measuring upper core, all ages, both genders. I measured 10-, 14- and 16-year-old boys and girls that were upper core.

With the ebook and thanks to my SiriusXM Radio show, people were now coming to see me to determine what their dominant core swing was. Many thought they were upper core before they even arrived. By Aug. 23, some 83 percent were upper core and by the end of 2018, a full 85 percent of my students had measured upper core. I measured two major champions in this time period, that were preparing for the PGA Tour Champions, and they both were upper core.

FINDING THE WRIGHT BALANCE

By the end of 2019, the last 322 players I had measured in a row were upper core and I was now at 90 percent of my students being upper core. I could have made some mistakes along the way, but in the beginning I never would have guessed after measuring almost 800 students, that the vast majority of my students would be upper core like me.

- Three characteristics of an upper-core swing are, the hips are not very rotated at impact, we stand up and come out of posture, and don't have a lot of forward shaft lean at impact.

- Guess what all the mid-core teachers wanted me to do? Rotate more, stay in posture, and get more forward shaft lean at impact.

- When I started blocking the ball to the right they wanted to strengthen my left-hand grip.

- I know now that my left-hand grip affects my ability to turn on the backswing, and a stronger or incorrect grip can limit my range of motion on the backswing.

- When it comes to club fitting and using a lie board to determine lie angle, once again the upper-core player does not get fit properly because we stand up and come out of posture, which results in our clubs sometimes being bent too upright.

- Upper-core players use vertical ground force more than anybody else. I was on my tippy toes in high school at impact and then later some teachers and players said I needed to swing through on a flat left foot. That one's been debunked.

THE JOURNEYMAN

Getting matched up is a big thing in teaching today. Things have to match up. That's what is so great about Wright Balance. Things match up whether you are a low-, mid- or upper-core player and Wright Balance Fitters can give you the correct stance widths so that you can do this naturally. Your stance widths determine your balance; balls of the feet, over the arches, or in between, and your balance determines what your body can and cannot do. I've seen amazing things since I started using this system.

At the end of the day, it doesn't matter how much technology you have, or what you've done in your life as a player or teacher. All that matters is, did you help someone? Did you help them to understand how their natural swing works? Did you help them to understand the ball flight laws? Did you help them to understand their misses so they could fix themselves out on the golf course? That's what I try to do every day. If there is something out there better than Wright Balance, I want to see it, because I'm now in the business of helping people.

At the 2019 PNC/Father Son, I got to sit in with Joe Don Rooney of Rascal Flatts. Peter Jacobsen was hosting, and came up and sang with us on "Love the One You Whiff," a Jake Trout and the Flounders song. It had been a long time since Jake and I had played together, and it was great. Friends are friends forever, if the Lord's the Lord of them.

Epilogue

There are only four players on the PGA Tour who have played in over 500 PGA Tour events without a win. They are listed in the order that they reached that milestone.

1. Bobby Wadkins 715 starts, 464 cuts
2. John Adams 566 starts, 280 cuts
3. Larry Rinker 525 starts, 283 cuts
4. Jay Delsing 565 starts, 276 cuts

Laurie, Lee, and Larry Rinker have more than 1,150 combined starts on the PGA Tour and LPGA Tour. We were considered Florida's first golf family.

Four Rinkers: Laurie, Lee, Larry, Laine Jr.

Bob Toski has always said that at the end of the day, life is about memories, and the friends we make. There are no time limits for success. You never fail until you quit. I want to thank my family and friends for the life that I have been able to live. So many people did so many things for me, and with a lot of them I will never ever be able to do for them what they did for me. Someone said you should never jump off of a roller coaster in the middle of the ride. I'm glad my ride isn't over. We were "The Journeymen."

Larry Rinker Professional Victories 1980-1995
All two- or more-day events

1980	4 victories on J.C. Goosie Space Coast Tour, Florida
	2 victories on Old Colony Bank Tour, Massachusetts
1981	1 victory First Stage of Tour School – Magnolia, Disney
1983	1 victory North Florida PGA Winter Tour, won in playoff
1984	1 Victory Gator Pro-Am – Gainesville, FL
1985	1 victory JC Penney Mixed Team Classic – Bardmoor CC
1992	1 victory British Open Qualifying – Luffness New
1995	1 victory J.C. Goosie Gary Player Tour – Kissimmee, Fla.
	1 victory Future Master Tour – Deer Island

Larry Rinker Junior and Amateur Victories

1974	Florida State Jaycee Junior, Lehigh Acres CC
1975	Western Junior Medalist, Stillwater, Okla.
1978	SEC Championship, Shoal Creek, Birmingham, Ala.

Appendix I

Green Augusta

By: Harvey Mason and Larry Rinker
Publishing: Masong Music, ASCAP; One Putt Music, B.M.I.

Turned into the garden, down Magnolia Lane
Walked around the clubhouse
you could feel the National fame
There was Arnie, Jack, and Tiger
making history once again
I can smell the pine, at
Green Augusta, Green Augusta,
Green Augusta, Green Augusta

Built by Mr. Jones and MacKenzie
in the north Georgia hills
Amidst the dogwood and azalea
pine trees and golden bell
Can't believe the beauty, why it's heaven on earth
A special place in time, it's forever on my mind
I can't wait to find,
Green Augusta, Green Augusta,
Green Augusta, Green Augusta

Prayed through Amen Corner, walked across Ben Hogan Bridge
While they were waitin' on the 13th Tee,
looked around at Rae's Creek again

I'm here at the Masters, livin' out Cliff's dream
It's been going on since 1934, it'll never never end
Green Augusta, Green Augusta,
Green Augusta, Green Augusta

Appendix II

Fly Away *(Payne's Song)*
By: Larry Rinker
Publishing: One Putt Music, B.M.I.

I remember the day we met, He was brave and confident
We were young and full of dreams
He liked to play for cash, And he liked to talk the trash
Now he's walkin' and a talkin' with the Lord above

had to fly fly fly away, had to fly fly fly away
had to fly fly fly away
I still miss him everyday

I didn't know God's plan, For Payne to take the stand
No one knew he'd be a Lamb of God
He was determined to win, Even when his faith was thin
Now he's walkin' in the clouds in the hands of God

had to fly fly fly away
had to fly fly fly away
had to fly fly fly away
I still miss him everyday

Hey man, thanks for helpin' me understand
That life's not perfect, so don't stop tryin', Cause it's not
And in these times, I try to find a little peace of mind
I believe it was his time, that's how I can calm my mind

I saw a hawk today, On the flag not far away
It reminded me of what my friend would say

Just learn to trust yourself, Or in God what else
Just know He gives you all you need

had to fly fly fly away, He had to fly fly fly away He had to fly fly fly away I still miss him everyday, I still miss him everyday